William Shakespeare, Homer Baxter Sprague

Shakespeare's Comedy of The Tempest

William Shakespeare, Homer Baxter Sprague

Shakespeare's Comedy of The Tempest

ISBN/EAN: 9783744774406

Printed in Europe, USA, Canada, Australia, Japan

Cover: Foto ©Thomas Meinert / pixelio.de

More available books at **www.hansebooks.com**

SHAKESPEARE'S

COMEDY OF

THE TEMPEST

EDITED WITH NOTES

BY

HOMER B. SPRAGUE, A.M., Ph.D.

FORMERLY PROFESSOR OF RHETORIC IN CORNELL UNIVERSITY; AFTERWARDS PRESIDENT
OF THE STATE UNIVERSITY OF NORTH DAKOTA; FOUNDER OF THE MARTHA'S
VINEYARD SUMMER INSTITUTE; LECTURER ON SHAKESPEARE, MILTON,
GOLDSMITH, ETC., UNDER THE AUSPICES OF THE AMERICAN SOCIETY
FOR THE EXTENSION OF UNIVERSITY TEACHING

WITH

SUGGESTIONS AND PLANS FOR STUDY, TOPICS FOR ESSAYS, ETC.

SILVER, BURDETT AND COMPANY
NEW YORK   BOSTON   CHICAGO

PREFACE.

THIS edition of Shakespeare's *The Tempest* is designed to meet especially the wants of teachers and students, but it is hoped that many others may find it useful. Of course all the notes will not be alike valuable to each, but probably nine of every ten readers will find in them something helpful.

If it be asked, "Why add another to the many school editions?" the following points of difference between it and most if not all of the other editions may be mentioned: —

1. The notes are intended to stimulate rather than supersede thought.

2. The results of many of the latest studies in interpretation by scholars have been given.

3. The edition continually presents for choice the various opinions of leading editors and commentators.

4. It suggests some of the best methods of studying English literature, and of making the finest passages the basis of lessons in language and rhetoric.

5. It contains critical comments by Assistant Professor Wendell, Dr. Furness, and other recent writers, as well as by Coleridge, Schlegel, and other geniuses of past generations; also topics for essays, and an unusually copious index.

6. Out of regard for the feelings of youth, it treats with more delicacy than most editions certain passages difficult to handle in mixed classes.

As in our edition of *Hamlet, Merchant of Venice, Macbeth, As You Like It, Midsummer Night's Dream,* and *Julius Cæsar,* we follow, in numbering the lines, the excellent edition of Dr. Rolfe.

To make the student's mastery of these dramas easy, complete, and delightful; to insure in him some appreciation of the richness of Shakespearian thought and the felicity of Shakespearian expression; to enlarge his vocabulary, sharpen his critical judgment, and store his memory with some of the choicest gems in literature; and so to multiply his sources of enjoyment and lift him to a higher plane of being, — these are some of the principal objects sought in this new school edition.

CONTENTS.

	PAGE
INTRODUCTION TO THE TEMPEST	9
TEXT, POSITION, LENGTH, UNITIES	9
DATE OF COMPOSITION; VERSE TESTS	9
SOURCE OF THE PLOT	10
CRITICAL COMMENTS	11

   Dryden. — Johnson. — Hazlitt. — Schlegel. — Coleridge. — Skottowe. — Mrs. Jameson. — Campbell. — Heine. — Lloyd. — Hugo. — Montégut. — Lowell. — Phillpotts. — Russell. — Furnivall. — Hudson. — Kemble. — White. — Garnett. — Furness. — Wendell.

	PAGE
EXPLANATIONS OF ABBREVIATED FORMS	22
THE TEMPEST — TEXT AND FOOT-NOTES	25
APPENDIX.	
HOW TO STUDY ENGLISH LITERATURE	133
SPECIMEN EXAMINATION PAPERS	139
TOPICS FOR ESSAYS	141
INDEX	143

INTRODUCTION.

THE EARLIEST TEXT of *The Tempest* is that of the First Folio (1623). It is printed there with remarkable correctness, according to Furness. Hudson declares, however, that "the play is badly printed, considerably worse than most of the plays first printed in that volume."

ITS POSITION is first in the Folio. It has been suggested that it was selected to occupy that place by the editors, Heminge and Condell, to make the book as attractive and salable as possible; that they put first in order the comedies, and, of the comedies, that one regarded as the greatest in charm, in beauty, in attractiveness.

IN LENGTH it is the shortest with one exception. *The Tempest* has 2064 lines; *The Comedy of Errors*, 1778.

THE UNITIES are all observed; place, time, and action. Herein it conforms more strictly to ancient classical rules than any other of the plays, except, perhaps, *The Comedy of Errors*.

DATE OF COMPOSITION.

After wading through what would be equivalent to some sixty or seventy close-packed pages of this, our edition of *The Tempest*, Furness, in his great *Variorum Edition*, concludes thus:—

"The *Date of the Composition* of *The Tempest* is assigned as follows: by Hunter, to 1596; by Knight, to 1602 or 1603; by Dyce, Staunton, after 1603; by Elze, to 1604; by Verplanck, to 1609; by Heraud, Fleay, Furnivall, to 1610; by Malone, Steevens, Collier, W. W. Lloyd, Halliwell, Grant White (ed. i), Keightley, Rev. John Hunter, W. A. Wright, Stokes, Hudson, A. W. Ward, D. Morris, to 1610–1611; by Chalmers, Tieck, Garnett, to 1613; by Holt, to 1614; by Capell (?), Farmer, Skottowe, Campbell, Bathurst, the Cowden-Clarkes, Phillpotts, Grant White (ed. ii), Deighton, a late, or the latest, play.

"The voice of the majority pronounces in favor of 1610–1611. Let us all, therefore, acquiesce, and henceforth be, in this regard, shut up in measureless content."

THE VERSE TESTS, introduced during recent years, curiously confirm the opinion that *The Tempest* was one of the last of Shakespeare's plays. For example: of *end-stopt* lines (lines in which the sense stops or partially stops at the end), the proportion to *run-on* lines (lines in which the sense runs on without break into the following verse) is, in the three plays which all admit to be among his earliest, *Love's Labor's Lost*, *Comedy of Errors*, and *Two Gentlemen of Verona*, as $18\frac{1}{2}$ to 1, $10\frac{1}{13}$ to 1, 10 to 1, respectively. But of end-stopt lines in the three plays which all concede to be among his very latest, *The Tempest*, *Cymbeline*, and *The Winter's Tale*, the proportion to run-on lines is but as $3\frac{1}{5}$ to 1, $2\frac{1}{2}$ to 1, and $2\frac{1}{4}$ to 1, respectively. In the earlier plays he is, so to speak, tied down to a particular kind of verse, that in which the sense stops or partially stops at the end; in the later plays he is free from that bondage, and this freedom conduces wonderfully to dramatic power.

The following comparison is significant: —

	No. of pentameter (5 measure) rhyming lines.	No. of pentameter (5 measure) blank verse lines.	No. of extra (11) syllable lines.	No. of run-on lines.
Love's Labor's Lost . . .	1028	579	4	1 in 18 +
The Tempest .	2	1458	33	1 in 3 +

SOURCE OF THE PLOT.

No source of the plot has been found. It is commonly thought that Shakespeare may have drawn it from some long-lost Italian novel.

A few of the incidents may have been suggested to him by the story of Sir George Somers.

It seems that in May, 1609, Sir George Somers sailed with a fleet of nine ships for Virginia. A terrible tempest scattered them in mid-ocean. Seven ships reached Virginia; but the *Sea Venture*, the admiral ship, was wrecked on one of the Bermuda islands, "a most prodigious and enchanted place, affording nothing but gusts, storms, and foul weather," "an enchanted pile of rocks, and a desert inhabitation of devils."

A pamphlet entitled *A Discovery of the Bermudas, otherwise called the Isle of Devils*, published in 1610, gave an account of this storm and wreck. The sailors, exhausted, had given up all hope and bid each other farewell, when the ship was found jammed between two rocks, so that all lives were saved. For nine months they lived there, and repaired their ship. They found the island a delightful place. The air was balmy, the fairies were birds, and the devils, wild hogs!

In John Holt's *An Attempte to Rescue that Annciente, English Poet, And Play-Wrighte, Williame Shakespeare, from the Maney Errours, faulsley charged on him, by Certaine New-fangled Wittes; And to let him Speak for Himself*, etc., published in 1749, the author, in speaking of the Masque in Act IV of *The Tempest*, where "Juno sings her blessings" on the young couple —

Honor, Riches, Marriage-Blessing —

suggests that this passage "may perhaps give a Mark to guess at the time this play was wrote; it appearing to be a compliment intended by the Poet, on some particular solemnity of that kind; and if so, none more likely than the contracting the young Earl of Essex, in 1606, with the Lady Frances Howard; which marriage was not attempted to be consummated, till the Earl returned from his travels four years afterwards; a circumstance which seems to be hinted at, in IV, i, 18; unless any one should choose to think it designed for the marriage of the Palsgrave with the Lady Elizabeth, King James's Daughter, in 1612. But the first seems to carry most weight with it as being a testimony of the Poet's gratitude to the then Lord Southampton, a warm Patron of the Author's, and as zealous a friend to the Essex family: In either case, it will appear, 't was one of the last Plays wrote by our Author, though it has stood the first in all the printed editions since 1623, which Preheminence given it by the Players is no bad Proof of its being the last, this Author furnished them with." — Quoted from *Furness*.

Tieck in 1817 discovered 'an analogue of *The Tempest*' in an old German Comedy, *Die schöne Sidea*, The Fair Sidea. Furness translates it in full (*Var. ed.* pp. 325-341), and shows the improbability that Shakespeare could have drawn from it.

CRITICAL COMMENTS.[1]

(From Dryden's Preface to Troilus and Cressida, 1679.)

To return once more to Shakespeare; no man ever drew so many characters, or generally distinguished 'em better from one another, excepting only *Jonson*: I will instance but one, to show the copiousness of his invention; 't is that of Calyban, or the monster in *The Tempest*. He seems there to have created a person which was not in Nature, a boldness which at first sight would appear intolerable; for he makes him a species of himself, begotten by an Incubus on a Witch;

---

[1] These comments are not selected with a view of presenting a complete treatment of any points or topics; but, rather, to awaken the reader's interest, and stimulate him to further investigation and independent judgment.

but this, as I have elsewhere prov'd, is not wholly beyond the bounds of credibility; at least the vulgar stile believe it. . . . Whether or no his generation can be defended, I leave to Philosophy; but of this I am certain, the Poet has most judiciously furnish'd him with a person, a language, and a character which will suit him both by Father's and Mother's side; he has all the discontents and malice of a Witch, and of a Devil; besides a convenient proportion of the deadly sins.

(From Johnson's Edition, 1773.)

Whatever might be Shakespeare's intention in forming or adopting the plot, he has made it instrumental to the production of many characters, diversified with boundless invention, and preserved with profound skill in nature, extensive knowledge of opinions, and accurate observation in life. In a single drama are here exhibited princes, courtiers, and sailors, all speaking in their real characters. There is the agency of airy spirits, and of an earthly goblin. The operations of magic, the tumults of a storm, the adventures of a desert island, the native effusion of untaught affection, the punishment of guilt, and the final happiness of the pair for whom our passions are equally interested.

(From William Hazlitt's Characters of Shakespeare's Plays, 1817.)

The Tempest is one of the most original and perfect of Shakespeare's productions, and he has shown in it all the variety of his powers. It is full of grace and grandeur. The human and imaginary characters, the dramatic and the grotesque, are blended together with the greatest art, and without any appearance of it. Though he has here given "to airy nothing a local habitation and a name," yet that part which is only the fantastic creation of his mind has the same palpable texture and coheres "semblably" with the rest. As the preternatural part has the air of reality, and almost haunts the imagination with a sense of truth, the real characters and events partake of the wildness of a dream. . . .

Even the local scenery is of a piece and character with the subject. Prospero's enchanted island seems to have risen up out of the sea; the airy music, the tempest-tossed vessel, the turbulent waves, all have the effect of the landscape background of some fine picture.

(From Schlegel's Lectures, 1815.)

In the zephyr-like Ariel the image of air is not to be mistaken; . . . as, on the other hand, Caliban signifies the heavy elements of earth. Yet they are neither of them allegorical personifications, but beings individually determined. In general, we find in *The Midsummer Night's Dream*, in *The Tempest*, in the magical part of *Macbeth*, and wherever Shakespeare avails himself of the popular belief in the invisible presence of spirits, and the possibility of coming in contact with them, a profound view of the inward life of Nature and her mysterious springs.

(From Coleridge's Lectures and Notes, 1818.)

With love, pure love, there is always an anxiety for the safety of the object, a disinterestedness by which it is distinguished from the counterfeits of its name. Compare *Romeo and Juliet*, Act II, Scene ii, with *The Tempest*, III, i. I do not know a more wonderful instance of Shakespeare's mastery, in playing a distinctly rememberable variation on the same remembered air, than in the transporting love confessions of Romeo and Juliet and Ferdinand and Miranda. There seems more passion in one, and more dignity in the other; yet you feel that the sweet girlish lingering and busy movement of Juliet, and the calmer and more maidenly fondness of Miranda, might easily pass into each other.

(From Skottowe's Life of Shakespeare, etc., 1824.)

The most decisive instance of the pre-eminence of Prospero as a magician is the obedience of Ariel. The necromancer of ordinary acquirements domineered over inferior spirits; the more skilful, over invisible beings of a more exalted nature; but that artist, alone, whose powerful genius had led him triumphant through the whole range of human science, could aspire to the control of spirits resident in the highest regions of spiritual existence.

(From Mrs. Jameson's Characteristics of Women, ed. ii, 1833.)

Let us imagine any other woman placed beside Miranda — even one of Shakespeare's own loveliest and sweetest creations — there is not one of them that could sustain the comparison for a moment; not one that would not appear somewhat coarse or artificial when brought into immediate contact with this pure child of nature, this "Eve of an enchanted Paradise."

What, then, has Shakespeare done? — "O wondrous skill and sweet wit of the man!" — he has removed Miranda far from all comparison with her own sex; he has placed her between the demi-demon of earth and the delicate spirit of air. The next step is into the ideal and supernatural; and the only being who approaches Miranda, with whom she can be contrasted, is Ariel. Beside the subtle essence of this ethereal sprite, this creature of elemental light and air, that "ran upon the winds, rode the curl'd clouds, and in the colors of the rainbow lived," Miranda herself appears a palpable reality, a woman, "breathing thoughtful breath," a woman, walking the earth in her mortal loveliness, with a heart as frail-strung, as passion-touched, as ever fluttered in a female bosom.

(From Campbell's Dramatic Works of Shakespeare, 1838.)

The Tempest, however, has a sort of sacredness as the last work of the mighty workman. Shakespeare, as if conscious that it would be his last, and as if inspired to typify himself, has made its hero a natural, a dignified, and benevolent magician, who could conjure up spirits from the vasty deep, and command supernatural agency by the most seemingly natural means. . . . And this final play of our poet has magic indeed; for what can be in simpler language than the courtship of Ferdinand and Miranda, and yet what can be more magical than the sympathy with which it subdues us? Here Shakespeare himself is Prospero, or rather the superior genius who commands both Prospero and Ariel. But the time was approaching when the potent sorcerer was to break his staff, and to bury it fathoms in the ocean — "deeper than ever did plummet sound." That staff has never been, and never will be, recovered.

(From Heine's Shakespeare's Mädchen und Frauen, 1839.)

. . . To what shall I compare you, Juliet and Miranda? I look up to the heavens and there seek your image. Perchance it lies behind the stars, where my gaze cannot penetrate. Perhaps if the glowing sun should have the mildness of the moon, I could compare it, Juliet, to thee! If the gentle moon should e'en have the ardor of the sun, I would compare it, Miranda, to thee!

(From W. W. Lloyd's Critical Essay, Singer's Second Edition, 1856.)

It is most curious to observe how many of the topics brought up by colonies and colonization are indicated and characterized by the play. — The wonders of the new lands, new races; the exaggerations of travellers, and their truths more strange than exaggeration; new natural phenomena, and superstitious suggestions of them; the perils of the sea and shipwrecks, the effect of such fatalities in awakening remorse for ill deeds, not unremembered because easily committed; the quarrels and mutinies of colonists for grudges new and old; the contests for authority of the leaders, and the greedy misdirection of industry while even subsistence is precarious; the theories of government for plantations, the imaginary and actual characteristics of man in the state of nature; the complications with the indigence; the resort, penalty or otherwise, to compelled labor; the reappearance on new soil of the vices of the older world; the contrast of moral and intellectual qualities between the civilized and the savage, with all the requirements of activity, promptitude, and vigor demanded for the efficient and successful administration of a settlement,—all these topics, problems, and conjunctures came up in the plantation of Virginia, by James I; and familiarity with them and their collateral dependence would heighten the sensibility of the audience to every scene of a play which presented them in contrasted guise, but in a manner that only the more distinctly brought them home to their cardinal bearings in the philosophy of society—of man.

(*From François-Victor Hugo's Œuvres Complètes de Shakespeare*, 1865.)

Many commentators agree in the belief that *The Tempest* is the last creation of Shakespeare. I will readily believe it. There is in *The Tempest* the solemn tone of a testament. It might be said that, before his death, the poet in this epopee of the ideal, had designed a codicil for the Future. In this enchanted isle, full of "sounds and sweet airs that give delight," we may expect to behold Utopia, the promised land of future generations, Paradise regained. Who in reality is Prospero, the king of the isle? Prospero is the shipwrecked sailor who reaches the port, the exile who regains his native land, he who from the depth of despair becomes all-powerful, the worker who by his science has tamed matter, Caliban, and by his genius the spirit, Ariel. Prospero is man, the master of Nature and the despot of destiny; he is the man-Providence!

The Tempest is the supreme denouement, dreamed by Shakespeare, for the bloody drama of Genesis. It is the expiation of the primordial crime. The region whither it transports us is the enchanted land where the sentence of damnation is absolved by clemency, and where reconciliation is ensured by amnesty to the fratricide. And, at the close of the piece, when the poet, touched by emotion, throws Antonio into the arms of Prospero, he has made Cain pardoned by Abel.

(*From Émile Montégut, in Revue des Deux Mondes*, 1865.)

The Tempest is clearly the last of Shakespeare's dramas, and, under the form of an allegory, is the dramatic last will and testament of the great poet, his adieux to that faithful public whose applause, during the short space of five and twenty years, he had gained for five and twenty masterpieces, and more than eleven others which, full of imagination and charm, would have made for any lesser mortal the most enviable of crowns; in a word, this drama is a poetic synthesis, or, as Prospero would express it in the language of a magician, it is a *microcosm* of that dramatic world which his imagination had created.

Although the last of Shakespeare's plays, it is in that volume placed first, because, like the emblematic frontispieces of antique books, it prepares the reader for the substance of all that follows. No other play will do this, none other is such a synthesis of all. . . . The whole Shakespearian world is brought before the imagination by the characters of Prospero, of Ariel, of Caliban, and of Miranda.

(From Lowell's Among my Books, 1870.)

There is scarce a play of Shakespeare's in which there is such a variety of character, none in which character has so little to do in the carrying on and development of the story. But consider for a moment, if ever the Imagination has been so embodied as in Prospero, the Fancy as in Ariel, the brute Understanding as in Caliban, who, the moment his poor wits are warmed with the glorious liquor of Stephano, plots rebellion against his natural lord, the higher Reason. Miranda is mere abstract Womanhood, as truly so before she sees Ferdinand as Eve before she was wakened to consciousness by the echo of her own nature coming back to her, the same, and yet not the same, from that of Adam. Ferdinand, again, is nothing more than Youth, compelled to drudge at something he despises, till the sacrifice of will and abnegation of self win him his ideal in Miranda. The subordinate personages are simply types; Sebastian and Antonio and Francisco, of the walking gentlemen who fill up a world. They are not characters in the same sense with Iago, Falstaff, Shallow, or Leontes; and it is curious how every one of them loses his way in this enchanted island of life, all the victims of one illusion after another, except Prospero, whose ministers are purely ideal. The whole play indeed is a succession of illusions, winding up with those solemn words of the great enchanter who had summoned to his service every shape of merriment or passion, every figure in the great tragic comedy of life, and who was now bidding farewell to the scene of his triumphs. For in Prospero shall we not recognize the artist himself, —

> "That did not better for his life provide
> Than public means which public manners breeds,
> Whence comes it that his name receives a brand," —

who has forfeited a shining place in the world's eye by devotion to his art, and who, turned adrift on the ocean of life on the leaky carcass of a boat, has shipwrecked on that Fortunate Island (as men always do who find their true vocation), where he is absolute lord, making all the powers of Nature serve him, but with Ariel and Caliban as special ministers?

(*From J. Surtees Phillpott's Rugby Edition*, 1876.)

Another poet had depicted a magical tempest with a shipwrecked prince cast upon an enchanted island, and there relieved and tended by a king's daughter. The pictures are both beautiful, but they are not the same, and their difference is as marked a feature in their beauty as their likeness. — If an uneducated person wished to understand the meaning of a poetical creation, or, in other words, to see in what the essential unity of a poem consisted, he could hardly do better than exchange the details in Homer's canvas (*Od.* vi, 244, 275, 310), piece by piece, for those in Shakespeare. . . .
There is a real resemblance, on the other hand, between the characters of Nausicaa and Miranda. Each stands before us as an ideal of maidenhood, while the depths of tenderness in each are half revealed to us by their expressions of pity and sympathy. . . . Yet for all its unrivalled simplicity, Miranda's character marks the growth in the conception of woman's relation to society since the epic times. Nausicaa is no free agent: she may have preferences, but she does not choose; with a Quaker-like simplicity we see her preparing for her wedding with the suitor of her father's choice. Shakespeare required for his Miranda an amount of self-assertion which to Nausicaa would have seemed indecorous.

(*From Edward R. Russell in Theological Review*, October 1876.)

. . . We have in Prospero a being capable of calling forth spirits, of causing storms and shipwrecks, miraculous escapes and supernatural restorations, and indeed of doing everything very much as the Deity can, according to the received theory of special providences. To him, in the seemingly cruel exercise of his power, his daughter Miranda makes appeal in the celebrated passage, spoken in sight of the shipwreck, beginning: "If by your art, my dearest father, you have put the wild waters in this roar, allay them." May we not consider the rest of the play an answer, as this passage is an echo, to the weary doubts of ages in the presence of calamities caused by Omnipotence, which seems malevolent in not having prevented them?

(*From Furnivall's Leopold Shakespeare Introduction*, 1877.)

No play brings out more clearly than *The Tempest* the Fourth-Period spirit (*i.e.* of Reunion, of Reconciliation, and Forgiveness), and Miranda evidently belongs to that time; she and her fellow, Perdita, being idealizations of the sweet country maidens whom Shakespeare would see about him in his renewed family life at Stratford. . . . Turn back to the First-Period Midsummer Night's Dream, and compare with its Stratford girls, stained with the tempers and vulgarities of their day, these Fourth-Period creations of pure beauty and refinement, all earth's loveliness filled with all angels' grace, and recognize what Shakespeare's growth has been. . . . The general consent of critics and readers identifiés Shakespeare, in the ripeness of his art and power, more with Prospero than with any other of his characters; just as the like consent identifies him, in his restless and unsettled state, in his style of less perfect art, with Hamlet.—When we compare Prospero's "We are such stuff as dreams are made of, and our little life is rounded with a sleep," with all the questionings and fears about the future life which perplexed and terrified Hamlet and Claudio, we may see what progress Shakespeare has himself made in soul. . . . Contrast, too, for a moment, Oberon's care for the lovers in the Dream, with the beautiful, tender feeling of Prospero for Miranda and Ferdinand here. He stands above them almost as a god, yet sharing their feelings and blessing them. Note, too, how his tenderness for Miranda revives in his words, "The fringed curtains of thine eyes advance," the lovely fancy of his youth, her "two blue windows faintly she upheaveth" (*Ven. and Ad.* 482). He has seized in Miranda, as in Perdita, on a new type of sweet country-girl unspoilt by town devices, and glorified it into a being fit for an angel's world. And as he links earth to heaven with Miranda, so he links earth to hell with Caliban.

(*From Hudson's Introduction to the Play*, 1879.)

The Tempest is on all hands regarded as one of Shakespeare's perfectest works. Some of his plays, I should say, have beams in their eyes; but this has hardly so much as a mote; or, if it have any motes, my own eyes are not clear enough to discern them. I dare not pronounce the work faultless, for this is too much to affirm of any human workmanship; but I venture to think that whatever faults it may have are such as criticism is hardly competent to specify. In the characters of Ariel, Miranda, and Caliban, we have three of the most unique and original conceptions that ever sprang from the wit of man. We can scarce imagine how the Ideal could be pushed further beyond Nature; yet we here find it clothed with all the truth and life of Nature. And the whole texture of incident and circumstance is framed in keeping with that Ideal; so that all the parts and particulars cohere together, mutually supporting and supported.

(*From Mrs. F. A. Kemble's Notes, etc.,* 1882.)

. . . It is not a little edifying to reflect how different Prospero's treatment of these young people's case would have been if, instead of only the most extraordinary of conjurers, he had been the most commonplace of scheming matrons of the present day. He, poor man, alarmed at the sudden conquest Ferdinand makes of his child, and perceiving that he must "this swift business uneasy make, lest too light winning make the prize light," can bethink himself of no better expedient than reducing the poor young prince into a sort of supplementary Caliban, a hewer of wood and drawer of water: now, a modern chaperon would merely have had to intimate to a well-trained modern young lady, that it would be as well not to give the young gentleman too much encouragement till his pretensions to the throne of Naples could really be made out (his straying about without any Duke of Newcastle, and very wet, was a good deal like a mere adventurer, you know); and I am pretty certain that the judicious mamma, or female guardian of Miss Penelope Smith, the fair British Islander who became Princess of Capua, pursued no other system of provocation by repression. An expert matrimonial schemer of the present day, I say, would have devised by these means a species of trial by torture for poor Ferdinand, to which his "sweating labour" as Prospero's patient log man would have been luxurious idleness.

(From Richard Grant White's Studies in Shakespeare, 1886.)

Nothing is clearer to me, the more I read and reflect upon his works, than that, after Shakespeare's first three or four years' experience as a poet and dramatist, he was entirely without even any art-purpose or aim whatever, and used his materials just as they came to his hand. . . . The *Tempest* conforms to the unities of time and place merely because the story made it convenient for the writer to observe them; The *Winter's Tale* defies them because its story made the observance of them very troublesome, and indeed almost, if not quite, impossible. There has been a great deal of ingenious speculation about Shakespeare's system of dramatic art. It is all unfounded, vague, and worthless. Shakespeare had no system of dramatic art.

(From Dr. Garnett's Irving Shakespeare, 1890.)

The *Tempest* is not one of those plays whose interest consists in strong dramatic situations. The course of the action is revealed from the first. Prospero is too manifestly the controlling spirit to arouse much concern for his fortunes. Ferdinand and Miranda are soon put out of their pain, and Ariel lies beyond the limits of humanity. The action is simple and uniform, and all occurrences are seen converging slowly towards their destined point. No play, perhaps, more perfectly combines intellectual satisfaction with imaginative pleasure. Above and behind the fascination of the plot and the poetry we behold

Power and Right evenly paired and working together, and the justification of Providence producing that sentiment of repose and acquiescence which is the object and test of every true work of art.

(*From Dr. Horace Howard Furness's Preface to Variorum Edition*, 1892.)

With the exception of *Hamlet* and *Julius Cæsar* no play has been more liberally annotated than *The Tempest*.

Unquestionably, a large portion of this attention from editors and critics must be owing to the enduring charm of the Play itself, dominated as it is by two such characters as Prospero and Ariel, whose names have become almost the symbols of an overruling, forgiving wisdom, and of an "embodied joy whose race has just begun."

There is yet a third character that shares with these two my profound wonder, and, as a work of art, my admiration. It is not Miranda, who, lovely as she is, is but a girl, and has taken no single step in that brave new world just dawning on the fringed curtains of her eyes. "To me," says Lady Martin, in a letter which I am kindly permitted to quote, "Miranda's *life* is all to come." We know, indeed, that to her latest hour she will be the top of admiration, but, as a present object, the present eye sees in her only the exquisite possibilities of her exquisite nature. In Caliban it is that Shakespeare has risen, I think, to the very height of creative power, and, by making what is absolutely unnatural thoroughly natural and consistent, has accomplished the impossible. Merely as a work of art, Caliban takes precedence, I think, even of Ariel.

The student will do well to read Browning's poem, *Caliban upon Setebos; or Natural Theology in the Island.* "The essence of the poem," says Furness, "lies in its alternative title, which sets forth the vague questionings of a keenly observant, but utterly untutored, mind in regard to the existence of an overruling power, the problem of evil, the mystery of pain, and the evidences of caprice, rather than of law, in the government of the world, — such restless longing for a solution of the mysteries of life as rise unbidden to the mind when looking on the ocean, at high noon, amid the full tide of summer life."

(*From Ass't Prof. Barrett Wendell's William Shakespeare*, 1894.)

The *Tempest* is a very great, very beautiful poem. As a poem one can hardly love or admire it too much. As a play, on the other hand, it is neither great nor effective. The reason is not far to seek: its motive is not primarily dramatic; the mood it would express is not that

of a playwright, but rather that of an allegorist or philosopher. . . .
The very complexity and the essential abstractness of the endlessly
suggestive, philosophic motive of the *Tempest* is reason enough why,
for all its power and beauty, the play should theatrically fail. Like
Cymbeline, though far less obtrusively, it contains too much. Like
Cymbeline it reveals itself at last as a colossal experiment, an attempt
to achieve an effect which, this time at least, is hopelessly beyond
human power. Less palpably than *Cymbeline*, but just as surely, the
Tempest finally seems laborious. . . . The motive of the *Tempest*
we have seen to be philosophic, or allegorical, or at least something
other than purely artistic. . . . This quality of deliberation, perhaps, typifies the fatal trouble. Creatively and technically powerful as
the *Tempest* is,— sustained, too, and simplified, and beautiful,— it has
throughout a relation to real life which we cannot feel unintentional.
In a spontaneous work of art, one feels that the relation of its truth to
the truth of life is not intended, but is rather the result of the essential veracity of the artist's observation and expression. In such an
effect as that of the *Tempest* one grows more and more to feel that,
for all its power, for all its mastery, for all its beauty, the play is really
a tremendous effort. . . . In *Cymbeline* we found what seemed a
deliberate attempt to assert artistic power at a moment when that
power was past the spontaneous vigor of maturity. Here, in the
Tempest, we find another such effort, more potent still. . . . His
motive is not really dramatic, nor even purely artistic; it is philosophic, allegorical, consciously and deliberately imaginative. His
faculty of creating character, as distinguished from constructing it, is
gone. All his power fails to make his great poem spontaneous, easy,
inevitable. Like *Cymbeline*, it remains a Titanic effort; and in an
artist like Shakespeare, effort implies creative decadence, — the fatal
approach of growing age.

EXPLANATIONS OF ABBREVIATED FORMS.

The abbreviations of the titles of books in the Bible and of Shakespeare's plays hardly need explanation.

Abbott, Abbott's *Shakespearian Grammar.*
Adj., adjective.
Adv., adverb.
Ar., Arabic.
A.S., Anglo-Saxon.
Beaum., Beaumont.
Brachet, Brachet's *French Etymological Dictionary.*
Celt., Celtic.
Cent., *Century* (Dictionary).
Class., *Classical* (Dictionary).
Comus, Milton's *Masque of Comus.*
Cot. Fr. Dict., Cotgrave's *French Dictionary.*
Dan., Danish.
Dict., *Dictionary.*
Dim. or dimin., diminutive.
Du., Dutch.
E., English or early.
Ed., edition.
E.E., Early English (about 1250–1350).
Etc., *et cetera*, and the rest.
Et seq., *et sequentia*, and the following.
Faerie Q., Spenser's *Fairy Queen.*
Fr., French.
Furness, Furness's *Variorum Edition.*
Gael., Gaelic.
G. or Germ., German.
H.G., High German.
Ib. or ibid., *ibidem*, in the same.
Icel., Icelandic.

Id., *idem*, the same.
I.e., *id est*, that is.
Int. Dict., Webster's *International Dictionary.*
Ital., Italian.
Lang., language.
Lat., Latin.
Maetz., Maetzner's *Englische Grammatik.*
Med. or Mediæv., Mediæval.
Mid. Eng., Middle English (about 1350–1550).
New Eng. Dict., Murray's *New English Dictionary.*
Nor. or Norw., Norwegian.
O., old.
Obs., obsolete.
Orig., original, or originally.
Par. Lost, *Paradise Lost.*
Par. Reg., *Paradise Regained.*
Per., person (in grammar).
Pers., Persian.
Phila., Philadelphia.
Pres., present (in grammar).
Q. v., *quod vide*, which see.
Schmidt, Schmidt's *Shakespeare Lexicon.*
S. or Sh. or Shakes., Shakespeare.
Sing., 'singular' (in grammar).
Skeat, Skeat's *Etymological Dictionary of the English Language.*
Span., Spanish.
Var. Ed., *Variorum Edition.*
W., Welsh.
Wb., Webster's *Dictionary.*
Worc., Worcester's *Dictionary.*

DRAMATIS PERSONÆ.

Alonso, King of Naples.
Sebastian, his brother.
Prospero, the right Duke of Milan.
Antonio, his brother, the usurping Duke of Milan.
Ferdinand, son to the King of Naples.
Gonzalo, an honest old Counsellor.
Adrian, } Lords.
Francisco,
Caliban, a savage and deformed Slave.

Trinculo, a Jester.
Stephano, a drunken Butler.
Master of a Ship, Boatswain, Mariners.
Miranda, daughter to Prospero.
Ariel, an airy Spirit.
Iris,
Ceres,
Juno, } presented by Spirits.
Nymphs,
Reapers,
Other Spirits attending on Prospero.

Scene: *A ship at sea: an uninhabited island.*

THE TEMPEST.

ACT I.

SCENE I. *On a Ship at Sea: a tempestuous noise of thunder and lightning heard.*

Enter a Ship-master *and* a Boatswain.

Master. Boatswain!
Boatswain. Here, master; what cheer?
Master. Good: speak to the mariners: fall to 't, yarely, or we run ourselves aground; bestir, bestir!   [*Exit.*

ACT I. SCENE I. 1. **Boatswain** (pronounced by all sailors bō-sn), A. S. *swain*, fr. Icel. *sveinn*, boy, servant. "The boatswain is to have charge of all the cordage, tackle, sails, fids (wooden pins), marline-spikes, needles, twine and sail-cloth, and rigging." Capt. John Smith's (*our* John Smith, founder of Virginia) *Accidence for Young Seamen*, 1626. — He has charge of the boats, colors, anchors, etc. — 2. **master.** He commands a merchant vessel as a captain does a ship of war. — **cheer** = outlook? encouraging prospect? See line 5. — Late Lat. *cara*, Old Fr. *chere*, face, appearance, look. See our *Mer. of Venice*, III, ii, 307. — *John*, xvi. 33. — 3. **Good** — evasive, like 'well,' 'let that go,' 'no matter for that' [Hudson]? 'I am glad you are at hand' [Phillpotts, Moberly, Furness]? 'my good fellow' [Dyce, White, Rolfe, Corson, Schmidt, Deighton, Meiklejohn, etc.]? — The 'cheer' was good if they bestirred themselves? not otherwise? — See lines 14 and 18; *Hamlet*, our edition, I, i, 70; *Wint. Tale*, V, i, 19; *Com. of Er.*, IV, iv, 22; *Rom. and Jul.*, I, v. 6; *Abbott*, 13. — Is there a sound of courtesy, a feeling of conciliation in the word? If so, would it be used vocatively by the master to his boatswain? — After *good* in the folio is a colon, which is generally supposed to be here equivalent to a comma. — **speak** = say? call upon, apply to, exhort, bid do their best [Schmidt]? — A notice to be ready for quick action? — **yarely.** A. S. *gearu*, Old Eng. *gearo*, ready, quick, prompt. *Skeat.* "In the next speech *yare*, as an imperative verb, is *be nimble*, or *be on the alert*." *Hudson*. *Yare* is an adjective in V, i, 224. Is it still used? — *g* becomes

Enter Mariners.

Boatswain. Heigh, my hearts! cheerly, cheerly, my hearts! yare, yare! Take in the topsail. Tend to the master's whistle. — Blow till thou burst thy wind, if room enough!

Enter Alonso, Sebastian, Antonio, Ferdinand, Gonzalo, *and others.*

Alonso. Good boatswain, have care. Where's the master? Play the men.
Boatswain. I pray now, keep below. 10
Antonio. Where is the master, boson?
Boatswain. Do you not hear him? You mar our labor. Keep your cabins; you do assist the storm.

---

y, as *geong,* young; *dæg,* day. 5. **hearts.** Sailors still say 'my hearties,' and like to be called 'hearts of oak.'
cheerly.[1] Adv.? So *angerly, wonderly; masterly* in "Thou dost speak masterly," *Twelfth N.*, II, iv, 22. See *Abbott,* 447. — What the sailors need is cheerful courage, vigilant attentiveness, and prompt energy. Is the ship driving parallel with the shore? — 6, 7. **yare.** So "Yare, yare, good Iras; quick!" *Ant. and Cleop.*, V, ii, 282. — **topsail.** Danger of capsizing? of grounding? — In a square-rigged vessel, the topsail is the one next above the lowermost sail. — "When the topsail is furled, the sails are snug, and they can defy the storm to burst its wind with blowing, if only there is sea-room enough; which, by the next order, we see there is not." *Phillpotts.* — In Pericles (III, i, 44, 45, 46), we read —

1 *Sailor.* Blow and split thyself!
2 *Sailor.* But sea-room, an the brine and cloudy billow kiss the moon, I care not.

— So in *Lear* (III, ii, 1), "Blow winds, and crack your cheeks." The allusion is to the manner in which the winds are represented in ancient pictures, with their cheeks puffed out [Mason, Hudson, Deighton]? The humor of the comparison to a horse (as in *1 Henry IV*, II, ii, 13) with short breath or diseased respiration, marks the self-reliance of the speaker [Phillpotts]? — **whistle.** They are said to have been sometimes of silver or even of gold. See *Furness.*
9. **Play the men.** So in *2 Samuel*, x, 12; in *Chapman, Marlow,* and elsewhere in *Shakespeare.* — In *Macbeth* and *Henry VIII*, Shakes. has *play the woman,* i.e. weep. In *Mer. of Venice,* "the painter *plays the spider,*" etc. — 11. **boson.** With Knight and White we here reproduce the orig. folio reading. 'This coarse flippant man,' Antonio, is supposed to shorten, sailor-like, *boatswain* to boson. Dyce, Furness, and others think the unsettled state of our early orthography sufficiently accounts for the 'boson.' — 13. **assist the storm.** How? — In *Pericles*, III, i, 19, we

[1] "Oft listening how the hounds and horn
Cheerly rouse the slumbering Morn."
—Milton's *L'Allegro*, 53, 54.

Gonzalo. Nay, good, be patient.
Boatswain. When the sea is. Hence! What cares these roarers for the name of king? To cabin! Silence! trouble us not. 17
Gonzalo. Good, yet remember whom thou hast aboard.
Boatswain. None that I love more than myself. You are a counsellor; if you can command these elements to silence, and work the peace of the present, we will not hand a rope more. Use your authority; if you cannot, give thanks you have lived so long, and make yourself ready in your cabin for the mischance of the hour, if it so hap. — Cheerly, good hearts! — Out of our way, I say. [*Exit.*
Gonzalo. I have great comfort from this fellow: methinks he hath no drowning mark upon him; his complexion is perfect gallows. Stand fast, good Fate, to his hanging! Make the rope of his destiny our cable, for our own doth little advantage! If he be not born to be hanged, our case is miserable. [*Exeunt.*

---

have, "Do not assist the storm." — 14. **good.** See line 3. — 15. **Hence!** The energetic brevity and bluntness of the boatswain are quite refreshing, as he orders king, duke, counsellor, etc., out of his way. We are quite in love with him. **cares.** Sailor blunder for *care?* "When the subject is as yet future ... the third person singular might be regarded as the normal inflection." *Abbott*, 335. See I, ii, 477; IV, i, 259. — So it is in Greek? — Old plural in *s*? — 16. **roarers.** 'Roarer' was a slang term for blustering bully? — See scene ii, 2. — **To cabin!** Shakes. very often omits *the;* but there is a special propriety in brevity here. See on line 15. — *Abbott*, 90. — 18. **Good.** See on line 3. — 21. **of the present.** In *Jul. Cæs.*, I, ii, 161, we have *for this present;* in *Macbeth*, I, v, 55, *this ignorant present.* So in *Prayer Book*, and in *1 Corinth.*, xv, 6. — **hand.** In *Winter's Tale*, II, iii, 62, *hand* = lay hostile hands on. — 24. **hap.** Used by Shakes. as verb and noun. — 25. **Out of our way.** "I have great comfort from this fellow" — a genuine old 'salt'! — 26. **I have great comfort,** etc. "Gonzalo, the only good man with the king, is the only man that preserves his cheerfulness on the wreck and his hope on the island." *Coleridge.* — 27. **no drowning mark.** See V, i, 217, 218. In *Two Gentlemen of V.*, I, i, 140, 141, we read of the ship,

"Which cannot perish having thee aboard,
Being destined to a drier death on shore."

— **complexion** = nature, native bent, aptitude [Hudson]? external appearance [Schmidt, Rolfe]? external appearance as indicative of disposition, character [Deighton]? constitution, or temperament, as shown by the outward appearance [Wright]? — See our ed. of *Julius C.*, I, ii, 127. — 28. **gallows.** Adjective, as in 'gallows-bird'? — **perfect gallows,** like 'perfect Richard,' in *King John*, I, i, 90. — A. S. *galga*, a cross, gibbet. — 29, 30. **doth** = causeth, worketh? or is the word an auxiliary? — **advantage** = profit (received), gain? yield profit, benefit? See our note on *the dram of eale*, in our ed. of *Hamlet*, I, iv, 36. — *Two Gent. Ver.*, III, ii, 42; *Sonnet*, cxxxii, 8.

Enter Boatswain.

Boatswain. Down with the topmast! yare! lower, lower! Bring her to try wi' the main-course. [*A cry within.*] A plague —— upon this howling! they are louder than the weather or our office. — 35

Enter SEBASTIAN, ANTONIO, *and* GONZALO.

Yet again! what do you here? Shall we give o'er, and drown? Have you a mind to sink?

Sebastian. A plague o' your throat, you bawling, blasphemous, incharitable dog!

Boatswain. Work you, then. 40

Antonio. Hang, cur! hang, you insolent noise-maker! We are less afraid to be drowned than thou art.

Gonzalo. I'll warrant him for drowning, though the ship were no stronger than a nutshell.

Boatswain. Lay her a-hold, a-hold! Set her two courses. Off to sea again; lay her off.

---

32. **Down with the topmast** = "Strike or lower the topmast down to the cap, as it holds wind and retards the ship; evidently the main topmast, as only one is mentioned." *Capt. E. K. Calver*, of the Royal Navy. The ships of the Elizabethan age had usually no topmast. Lord Mulgrave says, "The striking of the topmasts was a new invention in Shakespeare's time." — **lower** = lower away the topmast? — 33. **Bring her to try wi' the main-course** = see if she will bear the main-course (*i.e.*, mainsail), and whether it will be sufficient [Capt. Calver]? "'To try with the main-course' was a technical term for keeping close-hauled, and beating up into the eye of the wind when there was too strong a breeze blowing for a ship to carry her topsail." *Phillpotts.* — '*Try* (or *tried*) *with the main-course*' is found in Capt. John Smith's Sea Grammar (1627), Hakluyt's *Voyages* (1598), and Raleigh's (*i.e.*, Sir Walter Raleigh's) *Works* (describing a voyage in 1597). — A ship's 'courses' are her largest lower sails, "which contribute most to give her way through the water, and enable her to feel her helm and steer her course." *Holt.* — **A plague** ——. The long dash after 'plague' in the folio perhaps indicates some profanity or blasphemy. See 38, 39; V, i, 218. — 34. **weather** = storm? — 35. **office** = official calls or commands?

36. **Yet again!** — The boatswain is justly impatient? — 39. **incharitable**. Shakes. uses quite indiscriminately the prefix *un-* or *in-*. — *Abbott*, 442. — 41. **you whoreson, insolent**. Sailors are just as coarse to-day. — 43. **for drowning** = in respect to drowning [Wright, Hudson]? either *as regards or against* [Abbott, Rolfe, Meiklejohn, Deighton, Phillpotts]? — See Gonzalo's previous speech about drowning. — 45. **Lay her a-hold** = keep her to the wind, or as close to the wind as possible, so as to *hold* or keep to it? — **two courses** = foresail and mainsail? See on 33. — The folio reads, "Lay her a hold, a hold, set her two courses off to sea againe, lay her off." Capell retains this reading; but John Holt (1749) and all

Enter Mariners *wet.*

Mariners. All lost! to prayers, to prayers! all lost!
Boatswain. What! must our mouths be cold?
Gonzalo. The king and prince at prayers! Let's assist them,
For our case is as theirs.
Sebastian.   I'm out of patience.   50
Antonio. We are merely cheated of our lives by drunkards. —
This wide-chapp'd rascal, — would thou mightst lie drowning
The washing of ten tides!
Gonzalo.   He'll be hang'd yet,
Though every drop of water swear against it,
And gape at wid'st to glut him.

---

subsequent editors, except Capell, punctuate thus: "Lay her a hold, a hold; set her two courses; off to sea again; lay her off" — ".it being a command," says Holt, "to set these two larger sails in order to carry her off to sea again, she being too near the shore. To 'lay her a hold ' signifies to bring her to lie as near the wind as she can, in order to get clear of any points, or head of land."

48. must our mouths be cold = must we drown [Deighton]? drink sea-water instead of ardent spirits [Birch]? must we die [Rolfe, Furness]? — Their mouths had been pretty hot? See V, i, 218, 219. — 'Mortifying groans' cool the heart, *Mer. of Ven.*, I, i, 82. Allen thinks 'cold orisons' ('cowardly prayers') are contrasted with 'brave oaths,' as Beaumont and Fletcher have it in *The Sea Voyage*, I, i, an imitation of *The Tempest.* In I, ii, 220-222, sighs cool the air.

"Thou rascal, thou fearful rogue, thou hast been praying! . . .
To discourage our friends with your cold orisons?"

Phillpotts interprets thus: "You go to prayers; we'll stave some of the puncheons of liquor to warm our mouths." Hence Antonio, lines 51, 52, calls them drunkards. This interpretation would emphasize *our?* — See 'red-hot with drinking,' in IV, i, 171. — **51. merely** = simply? barely? absolutely? Lat. *merus* = pure, unmixed. — Shakes. often uses 'mere' and 'merely' in the sense of absolute, absolutely, as in *Hamlet*, I, ii, 137. So Bacon, *Essay* 58. — **52. wide-chapp'd** (wide-chopped) = opening the mouth wide [Schmidt, Meiklejohn]? — "Men with wide chops are weak and doltish." *Croft.* "As he opens his jaws to drink now, so may he have to drink the sea-water!" *Phillpotts.* Do not lines 34, 38, 41, and V, i, 218-220, suggest that it is his clamor, his open-mouthed *shouting*, that gives him the epithet? — **The washing of ten tides** = while ten tides ebb and flow? — Allusion to singular mode of execution of pirates in England in the olden time — hanged on the shore at low-water mark, there to remain till three tides had overflowed them? Cited by Elze from Harrison's *Description of England.* — Like "I would have him nine years a-killing," *Othello*, IV, i, 166. — **53, 54**, Gonzalo still believes "He that's born to be hanged will never be drowned"! — **55. glut.** Latin *glutire*, to swallow; *gula*, throat. Milton uses *glutted*, for swallowed, *Par. Lost*,

[*A confused noise within.* 'Mercy on us!' —
'We split, we split!' — 'Farewell, my wife and children!' —
'Farewell, brother!' — 'We split, we split, we split!' —] 57
Antonio. Let's all sink with the king. [*Exit.*
Sebastian. Let's take leave of him. [*Exit.*
Gonzalo. Now would I give a thousand furlongs of sea for an acre of barren ground; long heath, brown furze, any thing. The wills above be done! but I would fain die a dry death. [*Exit.*

---

x, 633. — 61. **long heath, brown furze.** Hanmer (1744) changed this to *ling, heath, broom, furz*. The change is approved by Farmer, Sidney Walker, Dyce, Wright, Hudson, Deighton, Phillpotts, etc. But Furness says as follows: "The insurmountable difficulty in accepting Hanmer's change is, to me, that 'Long Heath' is the real name of a plant, just as much as is 'Long Purples.'" He quotes from Lyte's *Herbal*, 1576: "There is in this country two kinds of Heath; one which beareth his flowers alongst the stems, and is called 'Long Heath.'" Furness adds: "In Hanmer's emendation the four names really represent only two plants. . . . In Shakespeare's time, as witness Lyte, 'ling' and 'heath' were the same, and 'furz' and 'broom' the same. Such a mere bare iteration, without adding anything whatsoever to the picture, grates me as somewhat un-Shakespearian.

Why is this scene mainly prose? — Why any blank verse? — What pictures are in the word-painting? — How did Shakespeare get his knowledge of technical sailor language and of the proper management of a ship? — What development thus far of characters? — What lesson is taught as to artificial rank? — Name from memory the successive positions of the ships and expedients resorted to.

Lord Mulgrave, a distinguished officer in the British naval service, communicated to Malone the following analysis of the succession of events in managing the ship, the orders given, etc., in the first scene: —

1ST POSITION.
Fall to 't yarely, or we run ourselves aground.

1ST POSITION.
Land discovered under the lee; the wind blowing too fresh to haul upon a wind with the topsail set. The first command is a notice to be ready to execute any orders briskly.

2D POSITION.
Yare, yare, take in the topsail; blow till thou burst thy wind, if room enough.

2D POSITION.
The topsail is taken in. The danger in a good sea-boat is only from being too near the land: this is introduced here to account for the next order.

3D POSITION.
Down with the topmast. Yare, lower, lower; bring her to try with the main course.

3D POSITION.
The gale increasing, the topmast is struck, to take the weight from aloft, make the ship drift less to leeward, and bear the mainsail under which the ship is laid to.

4TH POSITION.
Lay her a-hold, a-hold; set her two courses, off to sea again, lay her off.

4TH POSITION.
The ship, having driven near the shore, the mainsail is hauled up; the ship wore, and the two courses set on the other tack, to endeavor to clear the land that way.

Scene II. *The Island. Before Prospero's Cell.*

Enter Prospero *and* Miranda.

Miranda. If by your art, my dearest father, you have
Put the wild waters in this roar, allay them.
The sky, it seems, would pour down stinking pitch,
But that the sea, mounting to the welkin's cheek,
Dashes the fire out.   O, I have suffer'd
With those that I saw suffer!   A brave vessel,
Who had, no doubt, some noble creature in her,
Dash'd all to pieces.   O, the cry did knock

5th Position.	5th Position.
We split, we split.	The ship, not able to weather a point, is driven on shore.

Grey (in *Critical, Historical, and Explanatory Notes*), 1754, and Maginn (in *Fraser's Magazine*), 1839, call attention to extraordinary resemblances between this scene and the description of the tempest in *Rabelais*, Book IV, xviii–xxii, which had not been translated into English in Shakespeare's time.

Scene II.   Prospero is not Shakespeare, but the play is, in a certain measure, autobiographical. . . . It shows us, more than anything else, what the discipline of life had made of Shakespeare at fifty, — a fruit too fully matured to be suffered to hang much longer on the tree.   Conscious superiority untinged by arrogance, genial scorn for the mean and base, mercifulness into which contempt enters very largely, serenity excluding passionate affection while admitting tenderness, intellect overtopping morality, but in no way blighting or perverting it, — such are the mental features of him in whose development the man of the world had kept pace with the poet, and who now shone as the consummate example of both. — Garnett's *Irving Shakespeare*, 1890.

4. **welkin's.**   A. S. *wolken*, a cloud. — "Like a jewel in the ear of *cœlo*, the sky, the welkin, the heaven," *Love's Lab. L.*, IV, ii, 5. — **cheek.** Shakespeare is fond of this personification.   "The cloudy cheeks of heaven," *Richard II*, III, iii, 56. — 5. **Dashes.**   In *Mer. of Venice*, II, vii, 44, 45, we read of

> "The watery kingdom whose ambitious head
> Spits in the face of heaven."

See *Pericles*, III, i, 1–6. — **fire.**   Dissyllable?   The first 'fire' is such in *Julius C.*, III, i, 172, —

> "As *fire* drives out *fire*, so pity — pity
> Hath done this deed on Cæsar."

— Abbott, 480, says, "Fear, dear, fire, hour, your, four, and other monosyllables ending in *r* or *re*, preceded by a long vowel or diphthong, are frequently pronounced (in Shakespeare) as dissyllables." — 6. **brave.** Armoric *brav*, fine; Scotch *braw*, handsome.   III, ii, 99.   Milton (*Samson Agonistes*, 717) uses 'bravery' in the sense of splendor, fine dress. So Shakes. and Bacon. — 7. **Who** = which. — The ship is thought of as a person [Wright, Meiklejohn, etc.]? — **creature.**   Collective here [Fur-

Against my very heart! Poor souls, they perish'd!
Had I been any god of power, I would 10
Have sunk the sea within the earth, or ere
It should the good ship so have swallow'd and
The fraughting souls within her.
　　Prospero.　　　　　　Be collected;
No more amazement. Tell your piteous heart
There's no harm done.
　　Miranda.　　　　　　O, woe the day!
　　Prospero.　　　　　　　　No harm.
I have done nothing but in care of thee,
Of thee, my dear one, thee, my daughter, who
Art ignorant of what thou art, nought knowing
Of whence I am, nor that I am more better
Than Prospero, master of a full poor cell, 20
And thy no greater father.
　　Miranda.　　　　More to know
Did never meddle with my thoughts.
　　Prospero.　　　　　　'Tis time
I should inform thee farther. Lend thy hand,
And pluck my magic garment from me. — So.
Lie there, my art. — Wipe thou thine eyes; have comfort.
The direful spectacle of the wrack, which touch'd
The very virtue of compassion in thee,

---

ness]? — 10. **of power** = powerful? — 11. **or ere** = before ever? See *Ecclesiastes*, xii, 6. — *Ere* is added to *or* for emphasis [*Mætz.*, iii, 451; Abbott, 131; Wright, Rolfe, Furness, etc.]? "*Or*, in this sense, is a corruption of A. S. *ær* (Eng. *ere*) = before." *Abbott.* Like 'very, very,' 'verily, verily.' See V, i, 103; also our ed. of *Macbeth*, IV, iii, 173, and our *Hamlet*, I, ii, 147. — 13. **fraughting**. Cotgrave's *French and Eng. Dictionary* (1632) defines *freter*, 'to hire a ship of burden, and to fraught or load her, hired;' also '*freture*, a fraughting, loading, or furnishing of a (hired) ship.' — Swed. *frakt*; Dan. *fragt*, a cargo; *fragte*, to freight. — *Mer. of Venice*, II, viii, 30, has 'a vessel of our country, richly fraught.' — 15. **woe the day** = woe to the day? — 19. **Of whence**. Redundancy? — **more better.** Double comparatives and superlatives for greater emphasis are frequent in *Shakes.* See line 438; *Mer. of Ven.*, IV, i, 242. — 20. **full poor.** See line 155; also 395. — 22. **meddle with** = trouble = mix with [Stevens, Meiklejohn, Deighton]? mingle with, interfere with [Collier, Rolfe, Ritson]?

24. **So.** Spoken in soliloquy? to Miranda [Furness]? — 25. **Lie there, my art.** "At night, when he put off his gown, he used to say, 'Lie there, my Lord Treasurer.'" So says Thomas Fuller, in his *Holy State* (1642), of Lord Burleigh. — 26. **wrack.** Always so spelled in *Shakespeare.* See *Macbeth*, our ed., I, iii, 114. White remarks that "A delicate ear will perceive that something is lost in point of melody by the uncalled-for change of 'wrack' to *wreck*." — 27. **virtue** = the most efficacious

I have with such provision in mine art
So safely order'd, that there is no soul—
No, not so much perdition as an hair   30
Betid to any creature in the vessel
Which thou heard'st cry, which thou saw'st sink. Sit down;
For thou must now know farther.
　Miranda.　　　　　　　You have often
Begun to tell me what I am, but stopp'd
And left me to a bootless inquisition,
Concluding,—'Stay: not yet.'
　Prospero.　　　　　　The hour's now come;
The very minute bids thee ope thine ear:
Obey, and be attentive. Canst thou remember
A time before we came unto this cell?
I do not think thou canst, for then thou wast not   40
Out three years old.
　Miranda.　　　　Certainly, sir, I can.
　Prospero. By what? by any other house or person?
Of any thing the image tell me that
Hath kept with thy remembrance.
　Miranda.　　　　　　　'Tis far off,
And rather like a dream than an assurance
That my remembrance warrants. Had I not
Four or five women once that tended me?
　Prospero. Thou hadst, and more, Miranda. But how is it
That this lives in thy mind? What seest thou else
In the dark backward and abysm of time?   50

---

part—the energetic quality [Johnson]? essence, soul [Rolfe]?—28. **provision.** Dyce, quoting II, i, 295, changes this to '*prevision.*' Why is 'provision' better or worse?—29. **soul.** For 'soul,' Theobald suggested *foyle*; Capell, *loss*; Kenrick, *ill*; Holt, *soyl* (*i.e.* soil), approved by Dr. Johnson; Rowe, Pope, Hanmer, and Warburton, *soul lost*; Bailey, *evil*; Gould, *hurte*. The recent critics prefer, with Heath and Stevens, to regard the construction as an *anacoluthon*. The syntax seems designedly imperfect; but the word *perdition*, literally loss, makes the sense clear.—30. **hair.** "The tithe of a hair was never lost in my house before," *1 Henry IV*, III, iii, 53, 54.—31. **Betid.** A. S. *tidan*, to happen; Mid. Eng. *be-* or *bi-*, causing. *Be-* gives a transitive force.—32. **Which ... which.** Distribute.

35. **bootless.** A. S. *bōt* = profit.—**inquisition.** Lat. *in.* into; *quærĕre*, to seek; *inquisitio*, inquiry.—41. **Out** = beyond? out of? past [Abbott]? fully? quite?—47. **tended.** See line 6, sc. i.—50. **backward.** So 'inward' in *Sonnet* cxxviii, and *Meas. for Meas.*, III, ii, 117, and 'outward' in *Sonnet* lxix, are nouns.—**abysm**, Old French *abysme*, French *abîme*; from Greek ἄβυσσος, *abussos*, bottomless; fr. ἀ privative, and βύσσος, sea-bottom.

If thou remember'st aught ere thou cam'st here,
How thou cam'st here thou mayst.
Miranda. But that I do not.
Prospero. Twelve year since, Miranda, twelve year since,
Thy father was the Duke of Milan and
A prince of power.
Miranda. Sir, are not you my father?
Prospero. Thy mother was a piece of virtue, and
She said thou wast my daughter; and thy father
Was Duke of Milan; and his only heir
And princess no worse issued.
Miranda. O the heavens!
What foul play had we, that we came from thence? 60
Or blessed was 't we did.
Prospero. Both, both, my girl;
By foul play, as thou say'st, were we heav'd thence,
But blessedly holp hither.
Miranda. O, my heart bleeds
To think o' the teen that I have turn'd you to,
Which is from my remembrance! Please you, farther.

—53. **Twelve year.** "In the older stages of the language, year, goat, swine, etc., being neuter nouns, underwent no change in the nominative case of the plural number." *Morris* and *Skeat.*—The first '*year*' in this line is said to have the force of a dissyl. But is a dissyllable really necessary? The line has five accents without such splitting of 'year.' May we scan thus?

Twélve | year since | Mirán | da, twélve | year since.

Abbott (480) marks thus:—

Twelve yé | ar since | Mirán | da twélve | year since.

Furness well remarks, "By such a division and prolongation of 'year' an emphasis is imparted which does not befit the sense."—55. **Sir.** Respectful? Note that in this dialogue Miranda says *you*, Prospero says *thou*. Inference?—56. **piece of virtue** = sample or perfect specimen of virtue [Wright]? model, masterpiece, of virtue [Rolfe]? a portion of virtue itself—In *Ant. and Cleop.*, Augustus Cæsar calls his sister Octavia 'a piece of virtue.'—58. **And princess.** The folio has a semicolon after princess. Hence, Pope changed *and* to *a*. Many editors have adopted this emendation; but by erasing the semicolon we, perhaps, avoid the need of other change. Hanmer prints 'thou his only heir.' "No worse issued was his only heir and princess." *Furness*, after *Knight*. Judgment on these changes?—63. **holp.** Shakespeare uses *holp* 19 times; *helped*, 6.—*Abbott*, 343.—In *Luke*, i, 54, we read "He hath holpen his servant Israel." The tendency in Shakespeare's age was to drop the *-en*.
64. **teen** (A. S. *teona*, injury, wrong; accusation) = grief, sorrow, trouble?—65. **from** = away from [Rolfe, Wright]? out of [Phillpotts]? quite gone from [Meiklejohn]? In *Julius Cæs.*, II, i, 196, we have 'Quite from the main opinion he held once.' So *Macbeth*, our ed., III, i, 99,

SCENE II.]   *THE TEMPEST.*   35

Prospero. My brother, and thy uncle, call'd Antonio, —
I pray thee, mark me, — that a brother should
Be so perfidious! — he whom, next thyself,
Of all the world I lov'd, and to him put
The manage of my state; as at that time   70
Through all the signiories it was the first,
And Prospero the prime duke, being so reputed
In dignity, and, for the liberal arts,
Without a parallel; those being all my study,
The government I cast upon my brother,
And to my state grew stranger, being transported
And rapt in secret studies. — Thy false uncle —
Dost thou attend me?
    Miranda.   Sir, most heedfully.
    Prospero. Being once perfected how to grant suits,
How to deny them, who to advance, and who   80
To trash for overtopping, new created

131; and iv, 36. — 67. **My brother, and thy uncle.** Note here the long parenthesis extending from line 67 to *Thy false uncle*, line 77. Thoughts crowd upon his brain faster than his tongue can formulate them? Point out the anacolutha. — 70. **manage.** A technical term from horsemanship? So in *1 Henry IV*, II, iii, 45, *Mer. of Ven.*, III, iv, 25. — **as** = the fact being? — I call him perfidious because of what I am about to say. — *as at that time* = because then? Prof. G. Allen (Phila. Sh. Soc., 1864) in a very learned note argues strongly that the phrase 'as at that time' means almost or exactly *then*, the 'as' being redundant. He quotes 'as at this time,' which he says means *now* in the Prayer Book; thus: "Almighty God, who hast given us thy only-begotten Son to take our nature upon him, and *as at this time* to be born," etc. — 71. "Milan claims to be the first Duchy in Europe." *Botero* (1630). — **signiories** = states of northern Italy owing feudal obedience to the Holy Roman Empire. — Lat. *senior*, elder; Mediæval Latin, *senior*, lord; French *seigneur*, Ital. *signior*, a lord. — The Visconti of Milan were perpetual vicars of the Emperor in Italy. Robertson's *Charles V*. — **arts** = arts becoming a gentleman, tending to improve the mind [Schmidt]? — Technically the Lat. *artes liberales* were, in the Middle Ages, grammar, logic, rhetoric, arithmetic, geometry, music, and astronomy. In more recent times, history, philosophy, and those other branches usually required for the degree of Bachelor of Arts or Master of Arts, are included.

76. **state** = dignity? pomp? political body governed, body politic [Schmidt]? — 77. **rapt.** Lat. *rapere*, to seize, snatch away. — 80. **who.** "There is no doubt that 'who' was in Shakespeare's time frequently used for the objective case, as it still is colloquially." *Clark & Wright.* Abbott, 274. See line 231; IV, i, 4. — 81. **trash for overtopping.** "A blending of metaphors. 'Trash' refers to hunting, and 'overtop' to gardening, or, at least, it cannot refer to hunting." *Furness.* 'Trash' is defined by Schmidt, to lop, to crop. So Warburton and Steevens. White says "'trash' was hunting slang." Staunton says, "In the present day sportsmen check the speed of very fleet hounds by tying a rope, called a 'dog-trash,' round their necks, and letting them trail it," etc. — Icel.

The creatures that were mine, I say, or chang'd 'em,
Or else new form'd 'em; having both the key
Of officer and office, set all hearts i' the state
To what tune pleas'd his ear, that now he was
The ivy which had hid my princely trunk,
And suck'd my verdure out on 't. — Thou attend'st not.
  Miranda. O, good sir, I do!
  Prospero.   I pray thee, mark me.
I, thus neglecting worldly ends, all dedicated
To closeness and the bettering of my mind   90
With that which, but by being so retir'd,
O'er-priz'd all popular rate, in my false brother

---

tros, rubbish, leaves and twigs picked up and used for fuel; Norw. *tros*, fallen twigs, half-rotten branches easily broken. — 'Trash' means crashings; *i.e.*, bits *cracked* off. *Skeat.* — Shakes. turns nouns at will into verbs. If the metaphor suggests trees or plants, then the tallest, the one overtopping, is not cut off, but trashed, *i.e.*, its top beaten down or broken into twigs and dry branches, etc.? — If the metaphor suggests hunting dogs, then overtopping is outstripping? Visiting the Edinburgh High School in 1882, the present editor repeatedly heard the master call the boy at the head of his class the 'top boy'! — Choose between these interpretations! There's vegetation enough in lines 86, 87. But see *Othello*, II, i, 290; *Ant. and Cleop.*, IV, xii, 23, 24; and *Furness.* — 83. key = tuning-fork [Phillpotts]? tuning-key for the harpsichord, etc. [Wright, Rolfe, Hudson, etc.]? "I think the first and obvious meaning is the same as when we speak of the 'keys of office'; then, secondly, by the association of ideas, this 'key' suggested the 'time' which follows." *Furness.* Choose! — 84. **Of officer,** etc. *Abbott*, 497, marks desperately for scanning, thus: —

Of óffic | er, and óff | ice sét | all heárts | in the (i' th) státe.

Well? See on lines 103, 165. — 85. **that** = so that? Bacon in his *Essays* uses 'that' six or seven times for 'so that.' *Abbott*, 283. — 86, 87. **ivy ... suck'd.** The ivy was supposed parasitic. Erroneously? See Ellacombe's *Plant Lore of Shakespeare.* — **hid my princely trunk.** "I recollect hearing a traveller of poetic temperament expressing the kind of horror he felt in beholding on the banks of the Missouri an oak of prodigious size, which had been in a manner overpowered by an enormous wild grape-vine. The vine had clasped its huge folds round the trunk, and from thence had wound about every branch and twig, until the mighty tree had withered in its embrace. It seemed like Laocoön struggling ineffectually in the hideous coils of the monster Python." *Irving.* — 87. **on 't.** Often Shakes. uses *on* for *of*. *Abbott*, 182. So, now, in rapid familiar conversation? Allowable?

89. **I, thus,** etc. Scan. — **dedicated.** Shakes. often omits the *-d* or *-ed* after the *t* sound. See on line 148. — *Abbott*, 342. — 90. **closeness** = privacy, retirement, seclusion? In *Luke*, ix, 36; *Macbeth*, III, v, 7, and elsewhere in the Bible and Shakespeare, 'close' = secret. — Lat. *claudĕre*, to shut; *clausum*, an enclosed place; French *cloître;* Eng. *cloister*. 91. **but by being,** etc. = were it only for the retirement it procured me [Rolfe, Phillpotts]? except for the fact that they were so retired, or that I was so retired [Wright, Deighton, Meiklejohn Hudson]? — 92. **O'er-prized** = surpassed in value? — Lat. *pretium*, price. — **rate** = estimation? esteem?

Awak'd an evil nature; and my trust,
Like a good parent, did beget of him
A falsehood, in it's contrary as great
As my trust was; which had indeed no limit,
A confidence sans bound. He being thus lorded,
Not only with what my revenue yielded,
But what my power might else exact — like one
Who having into truth, by telling of it, 100
Made such a sinner of his memory,
To credit his own lie — he did believe
He was indeed the duke, out o' the substitution,
And executing the outward face of royalty,
With all prerogative; hence his ambition
Growing, — dost thou hear?

Does it mean that the value was greater than any of the people would have thought? or greater than popular applause or esteem would have been to him? — See II, i, 106. — 93. **Awak'd.** Shakes. uses this and never 'awoke,' nor 'woke.' Note the continual personification. — 94. **good parent,** etc. See the Latin adage, *Heroum filii noxæ*, 'heroes' sons no good!' The Greek proverb is substantially the same! So, aforetime, "Ministers' sons and deacons' daughters"! — 95. **it's.** See line 392. — *Its* was just coming into use. The folio (1623) has '*its*' once; '*it's*' 9 times; '*it*,' in a possessive sense, 14 times. King James's version of the Bible (1611) uses '*its*' once (*Levit.*, xxv, 5); Milton (1608–1674), 3 times; Florio's translation of *Montaigne* (1598), quite often. — **contrary** = opposite (nature) [Wright]? — 97. **sans.** Lat. *sine*, without; Old Fr. *sens*; Fr. *sans*. The poets tried hard to naturalize in England this convenient monosyllable. Thus Shakes. in *As You Like It*, II, vii, 166: 'Sans teeth, sans eyes, sans taste, sans everything.' — **lorded** = made a lord [Rolfe]? invested with lordship [Phillpotts]? invested as a lord [Deighton]? invested with the dignity and power of a lord [Wright]? — 98. **revenue.** Shakes. places the accent sometimes on the first and sometimes on the second syllable of this word.

100. **into truth.** 'Into' here has been changed to 'unto' by Warburton (1747) and nearly all subsequent editors, including among others Knight, Singer, White, Phillpotts, Rolfe, Hudson, Wright, and Meiklejohn; and their comments have been voluminous and vast. See *Furness*. "Shakespeare's own words, which all understand, are vastly to be preferred to any modification, which, however acceptable to him who proposes it, appears to be incomprehensible to all others." *Furness*. — Interpret thus: Having, by telling his lie (often), made his memory such a sinner (as to realities), that he credited his own lie into truth (*i.e.*, really believed his lie to be true), he believed he was, etc. — 102. *To credit his own lie into truth.* So Dr. South says, "Vice can never be praised into virtue." *Sermons*, ed. 1744. Supply *as* before *to*? Abbott, 281. — 103. **He was indeed.** It is hard to scan this line without making it an Alexandrine (twelve-syllabled), whereat Procrustean critics are greatly distressed. See on lines 83, 165. The fact is, Shakespeare was under no obligation to please the grammarians and prosodists of his own time, much less of subsequent ages. — 104. **face.** Latin *facies*, the shape, form, appearance; *facĕre*, to make. — 105. **prerogative** (Lat. *præ*, before; *rogare*, to ask; *prærogativus*, one who is

Miranda.   Your tale, sir, would cure deafness.
Prospero. To have no screen between this part he play'd
And him he play'd it for, he needs will be
Absolute Milan. Me, poor man!—my library
Was dukedom large enough. Of temporal royalties   110
He thinks me now incapable; confederates—
So dry he was for sway—wi' the King of Naples
To give him annual tribute, do him homage,
Subject his coronet to his crown, and bend
The dukedom yet unbow'd—alas, poor Milan!—
To most ignoble stooping.
   Miranda.   O the heavens!
   Prospero. Mark his condition, and the event; then tell me
If this might be a brother.
   Miranda.   I should sin
To think but nobly of my grandmother.
   Prospero.   Now the condition.   120
This king of Naples, being an enemy
To me inveterate, hearkens my brother's suit;
Which was, that he, in lieu o' the premises,
Of homage and I know not how much tribute,
Should presently extirpate me and mine

---

asked his opinion first) = special privilege? pre-eminent right by reason of office or position? Scan.
   106. **sir.** Line 55.—107. **screen.** Meaning Prospero [Daniel]?— 108. **him** = Antonio himself?—All was in Prospero's name, Antonio being the 'power behind the throne greater than the throne'? Antonio would not have even a nominal duke, Prospero, between him and 'the outward face of royalty'—between the assumed *rôle* and the reality? —109. **Milan.** Putting the name of the country or state for that of its ruler? Accent?—**me.** *Abbott*, 201.—111. **confederates.** Lat. *con*, together, with, *fœdus, fœderis*, a league, compact. In *Henry VIII*, I, ii, 3, 'confederacy' = conspiracy, plot.—112. **dry** = thirsty?
   117. **condition** = terms of compact with the King of Naples?—situation?—**event.** Lat. *e*, out, *venire*, to come.—118. **might** = could? *Abbott*, 312.—119. **but nobly**—merely nobly? otherwise than nobly? —*Abbott*, 122.—Is there here a subtle transfer of the quality of nobleness from its proper object to the process of thinking? Express the idea in plain prose.—120. **good wombs have borne bad sons.** Shakespeare might have thought of 'Sidney's sister, Pembroke's mother.'—122. **hearkens . . . suit.** So 'listening their fear,' *Macbeth*, II, ii, 28; 'listen great things,' *Julius C.*, IV, i, 41, etc.; *Comus*, 169.—*Abbott*, 129.—123. **lieu.** Lat. *locus*, Fr. *lieu*, place. See our ed. of *As You L. I.*, II, iii, 65.— **premises.** Lat. *præ*, before; *mittere*, to send; *præmissum*, thing already stated or premised.—*In lieu* of the premises. Technical phraseology? of logic? of law?—See *In lieu whereof*, *Mer. of Ven.*, IV, i, 401.— 125. **presently** = immediately? Often so in *Shakes.* See our ed. of

Out of the dukedom, and confer fair Milan,
With all the honors, on my brother; whereon,
A treacherous army levied, one midnight
Fated to the purpose, did Antonio open
The gates of Milan; and, i' the dead of darkness, 130
The ministers for the purpose hurried thence
Me and thy crying self.
 Miranda.   Alack, for pity!
I, not remembering how I cried out then,
Will cry it o'er again; it is a hint
That wrings my eyes to 't.
 Prospero.   Hear a little further,
And then I'll bring thee to the present business
Which now's upon 's; without the which this story
Were most impertinent.
 Miranda.   Wherefore did they not
That hour destroy us?
 Prospero.   Well demanded, wench;
My tale provokes that question. Dear, they durst not, 140
So dear the love my people bore me, nor set
A mark so bloody on the business, but
With colors fairer painted their foul ends.
In few, they hurried us aboard a bark,
Bore us some leagues to sea, where they prepar'd
A rotten carcass of a butt, not rigg'd,
Nor tackle, sail, nor mast; the very rats
Instinctively have quit it. There they hoist us,

Hamlet, II, ii, 578.—**131. ministers.** Lat. *minister*, servant; *minor*, less? So *master* is from Lat. *magis*, more; *magister*, master.—**134. hint** = suggestion? allusion? subject? cause? motive?—Dan. *ymte*, to whisper. The meaning is affected by O. Eng. *henten*, fr. A. S. *hentan*, to catch, seize. *Worc.*—**138. impertinent.** Lat. *in*, not; *pertinēre*, to pertain to, concern, be relevant.

139. wench. A. S. *wencle*, a maid? *wancol*, 'tottery,' shaky. The word was used to express fondness, with joking good-natured, simulated contempt; like 'little rogue'!—**144. In few.** So *Hamlet*, I, iii, 126, etc. —Lat. idiom? Lat. *paucis* (*verbis*) = in few (words).—**146. butt.** The folio has 'Butt.' Many, including White, Hudson, and Rolfe, have changed it to 'boat,' following Dryden's version and Rowe (1709). But a *butt* is perhaps the Italian *botto*, defined as a 'galliot,' the hull having 'very rounded ribs, very little *run* (nautical), and flattish bottom, the ribs joining the keel almost horizontally, a sort of tub of a thing.' *Nicholson*, approved by *Furness.*—We venture to suggest another interpretation as follows: Prospero is speaking in strong disgust, and he uses 'butt' simply in contempt, as sailors use *tub* or *scow*. A. S. *byt*, a cask.—**148. have quit.** In his vivid poetic imagination he lives over again the experience

To cry to the sea that roar'd to us; to sigh
To the winds, whose pity, sighing back again, 150
Did us but loving wrong.
　　Miranda. 　　　　　Alack, what trouble
Was I then to you!
　　Prospero. 　　　　　O, a cherubin
Thou wast, that did preserve me! Thou didst smile,
Infused with a fortitude from heaven,
When I have deck'd the sea with drops full salt,
Under my burthen groan'd; which rais'd in me
An undergoing stomach, to bear up
Against what should ensue.
　　Miranda. 　　　　　How came we ashore?
　　Prospero. By Providence divine
Some food we had and some fresh water that 160

---

of that dreadful night; the past is again present, and he says 'have quit'! But many of the prosy commentators change *have* to 'had'!—See the present for the past in line 205.—See 'Vision' in the treatises on rhetoric. —**quit.** See on 'dedicated,' line 89.—**hoist.** This may be for 'hoisted'? —III, i, 10; *Abbott*, 341, 342.—152. **cherubin.** Shakes. uses 'cherub' in *Hamlet*, IV, iii, 47; and 'cherubins' as the plural in *Mer. of Venice*, V, i, 62, etc.—155. **deck'd** = sprinkled (for 'degged') [Collier, Malone, Staunton, Singer, Dyce, White, Rolfe, Wright, Deighton, Phillpotts]? covered [Heath, Schmidt, Johnson, Meiklejohn]? adorned [Holt]?—Hanmer would read 'brack'd'; Warburton, 'mock'd'; Rann, 'dew'd'; Johnson (?), 'fleck'd'; Thos. White, 'eik'd'; Hudson, 'degg'd'; Bailey, 'leck'd.' We venture to suggest that all the emendations seem steps prose-ward; that the usual, if not uniform, sense of 'deck' in Shakes. is *adorn;* and that many times in Shakes. tears are *pearls*, as in Moore's *Light of the Harem*,[1]

　　" And precious their tears as that rain from the sky
　　Which turns into pearls as it falls in the sea."

In *Sonnet* xxxiv, 13, "Those tears are pearl"; in *Lucrece*, 1213, tears are 'brinish pearl'; in *Venus and Adonis* tears are 'like pearls in glass'; *King John*, II, i, 169, 'heaven-moving pearls'; *Two Gentlemen of Ver.*, II, i, 224, 'a sea of melting pearl which men call tears'; *Richard III*, IV, iv, 323, 324,

　　" Those liquid drops of tears that you have shed
　　Shall come again transformed to orient pearl ";

in *Lear*, IV, iii, 22, 'as pearls from diamonds dropped.' May not 'drops full salt' = pearls? See on line 397.

157. **undergoing**=enduring, sustaining?—**stomach** = stubborn resolution? courage?—See *Jul. Cæs.*, V, i, 65; *Henry V*, IV, iii, 35, etc. - *Cotgrave* (1611) defines *courage*, 'metall, spirit, hart, stomache.'—The stomach was supposed to be the seat of courage?—159. **Providence.** Then Prospero believes, like Roger Williams, in an overruling Providence?—Usually misprinted with a period after *divine*, following Pope

---

[1] Moore quotes from Richardson, 'The Nisan or drops of spring rain, which they believe to produce pearls, if they fall into shells.'

A noble Neapolitan, Gonzalo,
Out of his charity, who being then appointed
Master of this design, did give us, with
Rich garments, linens, stuffs, and necessaries,
Which since have steaded much. So, of his gentleness,
Knowing I lov'd my books, he furnish'd me,
From mine own library, with volumes that
I prize above my dukedom.
 Miranda.   Would I might
But ever see that man!
 Prospero.   Now I arise. —
Sit still, and hear the last of our sea-sorrow.   170
Here in this island we arriv'd; and here
Have I, thy schoolmaster, made thee more profit
Than other princess can, that have more time
For vainer hours, and tutors not so careful.
 Miranda. Heavens thank you for 't! And now, I pray
  you, sir,
For still 'tis beating in my mind, your reason
For raising this sea-storm?
 Prospero.   Know thus far forth:
By accident most strange, bountiful Fortune,

(1723). — 162. **who being,** etc. The syntax is confused; but the best critics, with few exceptions, allow it to stand unchanged. Pope, Hudson, Keightley, and some others omit *who.* — 165. **steaded** = stood in good stead, done much service, helped? — So *Mer. of Ven.*, I, iii, 6, etc. — As to the scansion of this line, and the attempts to compress it or cut it down to a pentameter, Furness well says, "These devices . . . recall the attempts of the elder sister to squeeze her foot into Cinderella's slipper." See on lines 83, 103. — 169. **ever** = sometime? — at any time? forever? — *Abbott,* 39. — **arise** = get up (to give orders to Ariel) [Heath]? get up (a mere casual remark) [Capell]? arise in my narration, my store heightens in its consequence (as the interest of a drama rises or declines) [Stevens, Warburton]? the crisis of my fortunes has come (and I emerge from obscurity) [Wright, Hudson, Joseph Crosby]? arise (to put mantle on again) [Dyce, Delius, Collier, Rolfe, Br. Nicholson]? Staunton thinks the words *Now I arise* 'are spoken to Ariel, above.' Furness inclines to think them figurative. Guess again! — May there not be an astrological allusion? See lines 181, 182. — 172. **schoolmaster.** Shakes. repeatedly uses this word to denote a private tutor. *Tam. of Shr.*, I, i, 94, 129, 162; *Ant. and Cleop.*, III, xii, 2. — **profit** = benefit (received)? receive benefit [Wright, Hudson, Rolfe, Deighton]? — 173. **princess.** "The plural and possessive cases of nouns of which the singular ends in *s, se, ss, ce,* and *ge,* are frequently written, and still more frequently pronounced, without the additional syllable." *Abbott,* 471. "It is sufficient for a word to terminate in the sound of *s* to be regarded by the ear (*sic*) as a plural." *Furness.* — Rowe, Capell, Stevens, Malone, White, etc., change the word to 'princes.' — 176. **beating** = working violently [Wright]? throbbing [Deighton]? —

Now my dear lady, hath mine enemies
Brought to this shore; and by my prescience   180
I find my zenith doth depend upon
A most auspicious star, whose influence
If now I court not but omit, my fortunes
Will ever after droop.   Here cease more questions:
Thou art inclin'd to sleep ; 'tis a good dulness,
And give it way. — I know thou canst not choose. —
Come away, servant, come!   I am ready now;
Approach, my Ariel, come!

Enter ARIEL.

Ariel. All hail, great master! grave sir, hail! I come
To answer thy best pleasure; be 't to fly,   190
To swim, to dive into the fire, to ride
On the curl'd clouds, to thy strong bidding task
Ariel and all his quality.
  Prospero.   Hast thou, spirit,
Perform'd to point the tempest that I bade thee?

---

181. **zenith.** Span. *zenit*, a corruption of Arab. *samt*, way, road, path; Arabic *samt-ur-ras*, the way overhead. Figuratively, highest success? — As to the influence of the stars, see what Gloster and Edmund say in *Lear*, I, ii, 94-130. — 182. **influence.** Astrological? Lat. *in*, upon; *fluere*, to flow. *Job*, xxxviii, 31. — Milton's *L'Allegro*, 121, 122. — 183. **fortunes**, etc. See *Jul. Cæs.*, IV, iii, 216-222. — 185. **inclined.** Effect of Prospero's magic?

Miranda has dwelt alone, from her infancy, with her father on a desert island compassed by ocean and the heavens; and thus she has lived, fearless and delighted, in the midst of mystery and beauty. Quiet in the soul-sleep of innocence, trustful in her father's care and power, she has dread of nothing. The spirits of air are her ministers, the brutes of earth are meek to her, and even Caliban bends to her service. But clouds gather in the sky; winds rush upon the sea; with the storm comes her prince, and with the prince comes love. The visionary world is broken into by the actual; realities intrude on fancies; and out of dreams she merges into passion. Now this, — a fable in outward fact, — is a truth in the inward life. The actual, natural, genuine maiden *does* dwell much alone. Her life is an island full of enchantments, girded by immensity. Giles's *Human Life in Shakespeare*, 1868.

190. **answer**, etc. Neatly imitated by Fletcher in *The Faithful Shepherdess*. Milton evidently has it, and lines 252-254, in mind in *Paradise Lost*, I, 150-152, where Beelzebub speaks of possible service to the Almighty,

" whate'er his business be,
Here in the heart of hell to work in fire
Or do his errands in the gloomy deep."

— 193. **quality** = ability, power [Rolfe]? professional skill [Wright]? fellow-spirits, 'profession' [Steevens, Malone, Dyce, Hudson, Deighton, Phillpotts, Furness]? — 194. **to point** = to the minutest article [Steevens, Schmidt]? — **to** = up to, in proportion to, according to [Abbott, 187]? —

Ariel. To every article.
I boarded the king's ship; now on the beak,
Now in the waist, the deck, in every cabin,
I flam'd amazement: sometime I'd divide,
And burn in many places; on the topmast,
The yards, and bowsprit, would I flame distinctly, 200
Then meet and join. Jove's lightnings, the precursors
O' the dreadful thunder-claps, more momentary
And sight-outrunning were not; the fire and cracks
Of sulphurous roaring the most mighty Neptune
Seem to besiege, and make his bold waves tremble,
Yea, his dread trident shake.
  Prospero.   My brave spirit!
Who was so firm, so constant, that this coil
Would not infect his reason?
  Ariel.   Not a soul
But felt a fever of the mad, and play'd
Some tricks of desperation. All but mariners 210
Plung'd in the foaming brine, and quit the vessel,
Then all afire with me: the king's son, Ferdinand,
With hair up-staring,—then like reeds, not hair,—
Was the first man that leap'd; cried, 'Hell is empty,
And all the devils are here.'

Lat. *ad*, to; *punctum*, point; Fr. *de tout point.*—See *at a point* in our *Macbeth*, IV, iii, 135.—197. **waist** = between the quarter-deck and the forecastle [Johnson]?—198. **divide**, etc. "I do remember that in the great and boisterous storm . . . in the night there came upon the top of our main yard and main mast a certain little light, much like unto the light of a little candle, which the Spaniards call the *Cuerpo santo*, and said it was S. Elmo. . . . This light continued aboard our ship about three hours, flying from mast to mast and from top to top, and sometime it would be in two or three places at once." *Hakluyt's Voyages*, ed. of 1598, de Robert Tomson's voyage in 1555.—See 'Saint Elmo's fire' in the unabridged *Dict.*—Vergil's *Æneid*, ii, 682-684.—200. **distinctly** = separately [Staunton]?—Lat. *dis*, apart, *stinguĕre*, to prick.—202. **momentary** = lasting but a moment [Wright, Schmidt]? happening every moment? both senses?—204-206. **Neptune . . . trident.** See *Class. Dict.*—207. **constant** = composed? Lat. *constans*, steadfast, steady.—See our *Mer. of Ven.*, III, ii, 242.—**coil.** Celtic *goill*, a struggle. See our *Hamlet*, III, i, 67.—209. **of the mad** = such as madmen feel [Steevens, Hudson]? of delirium [Rolfe, Meiklejohn, Phillpotts]?—212. **afire.** *Abbott*, 24.—**Ferdinand**, etc. Dramatic skill shown in separating him from the rest?
  213. **up-staring.** Lat. *stare*, to stand; root *sta-*, to stand, be fixed, stiff. *Abbott*, 429.—See *Jul. Cæs.*, IV, iii, 278, where Brutus says to the ghost of Cæsar,

> " Art thou some god, some angel, or some devil,
> That mak'st my blood cold and my hair to stare?"—

Prospero.   Why, that's my spirit!
But was not this nigh shore?
   Ariel.   Close by, my master.
   Prospero. But are they, Ariel, safe?
   Ariel.   Not a hair perish'd;
On their sustaining garments not a blemish,
But fresher than before: and, as thou bad'st me,
In troops I have dispers'd them 'bout the isle   220
The king's son have I landed by himself;
Whom I left cooling of the air with sighs
In an odd angle of the isle, and sitting,
His arms in this sad knot.
   Prospero.   Of the king's ship,
The mariners, say how thou hast dispos'd,
And all the rest o' the fleet.
   Ariel.   Safely in harbor
Is the king's ship; in the deep nook, where once
Thou call'dst me up at midnight to fetch dew
From the still-vex'd Bermoothes, there she's hid;
The mariners all under hatches stow'd,   230
Who, with a charm join'd to their suffer'd labor,
I have left asleep; and for the rest o' the fleet,
Which I dispers'd, they all have met again,
And are upon the Mediterranean flote,
Bound sadly home for Naples,
Supposing that they saw the king's ship wrack'd,
And his great person perish.

---

217. **are they, Ariel, safe?** Why this question? Did he not know? — 218. **sustaining** = bearing up or supporting the wearers [Steevens, Wright, Meiklejohn]? bearing or resisting the effects of water [Mason, Schmidt, Rolfe]? — Spedding and Hudson would read 'unstaining.' — See II, i, 61–63; also *Hamlet*, IV, vii, 174, 175, 180, 181. — 222. **cooling of the air with sighs.** See I, i, 48. — After 'cooling,' the 'of' indicates that 'cooling' is a verbal noun originally, as if it were 'a-cooling,' or (in the act) of cooling. *Abbott*, 178. — 223. **odd angle** = singular nook? out-of-the-way corner? — See 'odd' in V, i, 255. — 224. **knot** = folded form [Hudson, Wright, Rolfe]? *Hamlet*, I, v, 174. — 224–226, etc. Three things are inquired after. Note that Ariel's answer takes these up in their order. Hence the folio is right in placing a comma after *ship?* — 229. **Bermoothes.** See in the *Introduction*, under *Source of the Plot*, as to 'A Discovery of the Bermudas,' etc. — *still-vex'd Bermoothes* = the ever-chafed Bermudas? "Here," says Hanmer, "we have the Spanish pronunciation." In Elizabethan English, and for a hundred years later, 'still' often = *ever*. See our *Mer. of Ven.*, I, i, 17; our *Jul. Cæs.*, I, ii, 238, etc. — 231. **who.** See on line 80, IV, i, 4. — 232. **for the rest.** 'For' is still occasionally equivalent to *us for*. *Abbott*, 149. — 234. **flote.**

Prospero.   Ariel, thy charge
Exactly is perform'd; but there's more work.
What is the time o' the day?
    Ariel.   Past the mid season.
    Prospero. At least two glasses: the time 'twixt six and now
Must by us both be spent most preciously.   241
    Ariel. Is there more toil? Since thou dost give me pains,
Let me remember thee what thou hast promis'd,
Which is not yet perform'd me.
    Prospero.   How now? moody?
What is 't thou canst demand?
    Ariel.   My liberty.
    Prospero. Before the time be out? no more!
    Ariel.   I prithee,
Remember I have done thee worthy service;
Told thee no lies, made no mistakings, serv'd
Without or grudge or grumblings. Thou didst promise
To bate me a full year.
    Prospero.   Dost thou forget   250
From what a torment I did free thee?
    Ariel.   No.
    Prospero. Thou dost; and think'st it much to tread the ooze
Of the salt deep,
To run upon the sharp wind of the north,
To do me business in the veins o' the earth
When it is bak'd with frost.

Lat. *fluctus*; Lat. *flu-ĕre*, to flow; A. S. *flot*; Fr. *flot*, wave. — 240. **glasses** = hour-glasses = hours? half-hours? See on V, i, 223. — 242. **pains** = labor, care, trouble? — 243. **remember**. Lat. *re*, again; *memorari*, to make mindful of? make mention of? — Often used transitively in *Shakes*. — Line 403. — 244. **me**. So *me* in line 255. Old dative denoting that *to* or *for* which? — *Abbott*, 220.

    As a contrast to Caliban, we have Ariel, but by no means a purely ethereal, expressionless angel; rather a genuine spirit of air and of pleasure, graceful and free-thoughted, but light withal, mischievous, and at times a wee bit naughty. . . . Accordingly, almost like a human being, he has not infrequently to be reminded of it and kept in check. Franz Horn's *Schauspiele Erläutert*, 1832.

    249. **grudge** = complaint, murmur [Wright, Rolfe, Meiklejohn]? repining [Deighton]? grudging [Schmidt]? — Gr. γρῦ, gru, grunt of a pig. Imitative. Icel. *krutr*, a murmur; Swed. *kruttla*, Mid. Eng. *grucchen*, to murmur. — 250. **bate** = remit, deduct [Schmidt]? See II, i, 97, and our *Mer. of Ven.*, I, iii, 114. — 252. **ooze.** See III, iii, 100. — 253. **run.** *Isaiah*, xl, 31. — 254. **business.** See on 190.

Ariel. I do not, sir.
Prospero. Thou liest, malignant thing! Hast thou
  forgot
The foul witch Sycorax, who with age and envy
Was grown into a hoop? hast thou forgot her?
Ariel. No, sir.
Prospero. Thou hast. Where was she born? speak;
  tell me.
Ariel. Sir, in Argier.
Prospero. O, was she so? I must 261
Once in a month recount what thou hast been,
Which thou forget'st. This damn'd witch Sycorax,
For mischiefs manifold and sorceries terrible
To enter human hearing, from Argier,
Thou know'st, was banish'd; for one thing she did
They would not take her life. Is not this true?
Ariel. Ay, sir.

---

257. **liest.** Needlessly harsh? — **malignant.** Any relevancy in Johnson's remark that the fallen spirits, over whom magicians had power, were ill disposed?

With all our admiration and sympathy with the illustrious magician, we perforce must acknowledge Prospero to be of a revengeful nature. He has not the true social wisdom; and he only learns Christian wisdom from his servant Ariel. By nature he is a selfish aristocrat. When he was Duke of Milan he gave himself up to his favorite indulgence of study and retired leisure, yet expected to preserve his state and authority. When master of the Magic Island, he is stern and domineering, lording it over his sprite subjects and ruling them with a wand of rigor. He comes there and takes possession of the territory with all the coolness of a usurper; he assumes despotic sway, and stops only short of absolute unmitigated tyranny. Charles Cowden Clarke's *Shakespeare Characters*, 1863.

258. **Sycorax.** Stephen Batman (1537-1587) is quoted by Douce thus: "The raven is called *corvus* of *Corax*. . . . It is sayd that ravens birdes be fed with the deaw of heaven all the time that they have no blacke feathers by benefite of age." See lines 320, 321. — Among possible derivations of the word *Sycorax* are the following: ψυχορρήξ, Psychorrex (from ψυχή, psyche, soul, and ῥήγνυμαι, regnumai, to break); σῦκον, sukon, fig, and ῥάξ, rax, a poisonous spider, meaning Queen Elizabeth! Gr. σῦς, sus, ὗς, hus, a swine; κόραξ, corax, a raven; hog-raven, being a foul witch! [Gr. ὕαινα, huaina, hyæna, is properly a sow; then a Libyan wild beast. See on line 269.] — Arabic *Shokoreth*, deceiver. Seiaxghirir, a town on the island of Pantalaria, which, Elze thinks, is the possible 'original of Prospero's isle!' — See *Furness*. — **envy.** Lat. *in*, against; *videre*, to look; *invidia*, envy; hatred. — Often in *Shakes*. it denotes malice. — 261. **Argier.** Spanish and Port. *Argel*. The modern name, Algiers, dates from the 'Restoration'? The city has about 70,000 inhabitants. — 266. **one thing she did,** etc. But what it was, no person can tell. Perhaps Shakes. himself did not know! See *Furness*.

Prospero. This blue-eyed hag was hither brought with child,
And here was left by the sailors. Thou, my slave, 270
As thou report'st thyself, wast then her servant;
And, for thou wast a spirit too delicate
To act her earthy and abhorr'd commands,
Refusing her grand hests, she did confine thee,
By help of her more potent ministers,
And in her most unmitigable rage,
Into a cloven pine; within which rift
Imprison'd thou didst painfully remain
A dozen years; within which space she died,
And left thee there, where thou didst vent thy groans 280
As fast as mill-wheels strike. Then was this island —
Save for the son that she did litter here,
A freckled whelp, hag-born — not honor'd with
A human shape.
  Ariel.   Yes, Caliban her son.
  Prospero. Dull thing, I say so; he, that Caliban,
Whom now I keep in service. Thou best know'st
What torment I did find thee in; thy groans
Did make wolves howl, and penetrate the breasts
Of ever-angry bears. It was a torment
To lay upon the damn'd, which Sycorax 290
Could not again undo; it was mine art,
When I arriv'd and heard thee, that made gape
The pine, and let thee out.

---

269. **blue-eyed** = having a blueness, a black circle about the eyes [Schmidt]? the eyelids having a livid color [Wright]? Hyenas have blue eyes! (See on 258.)

"Woe to the half dead wretch that meets
The glaring of those large blue eyes
Amid the darkness of the streets!"
   — Moore's *Paradise and the Peri.*

So have some angelic women!

"Feeling or thought that was not true
Ne'er made less beautiful the blue
Unclouded heaven of her eyes!" — *Lowell.*

272. **And for thou wast.** Abbott, 151, remarks, "' For,' in the sense of 'because of,' is found not only governing a noun, but also governing a clause." — 274. **hests.** See III, i, 37; IV, i, 65. A. S. *haes*, a command. 277. **into.** Motion implied? *Abbott*, 159. — See line 359. — 284. **Caliban.** Coined by metathesis from *canibal* (cannibal)? Arabic *kalebon*, a dog? — Furness thinks Elze's suggestion more plausible, that the name is derived 'from the region called Calibia on the Moorish coast.'— 285. **Dull.**

Ariel.   I thank thee, master.
Prospero. If thou more murmur'st, I will rend an oak,
And peg thee in his knotty entrails till
Thou hast howl'd away twelve winters.
Ariel.   Pardon, master;
I will be correspondent to command,
And do my spriting gently.
Prospero.   Do so, and after two days
I will discharge thee.
Ariel.   That's my noble master!
What shall I do? say what; what shall I do?   300
Prospero. Go make thyself like a nymph o' the sea; be subject
To no sight but thine and mine, invisible
To every eyeball else. Go, take this shape,
And hither come in 't; go, hence with diligence!—
                              [*Exit Ariel.*
Awake, dear heart, awake! thou hast slept well;
Awake!
Miranda. The strangeness of your story put
Heaviness in me.
Prospero.   Shake it off. Come on;
We'll visit Caliban my slave, who never
Yields us kind answer.
Miranda.   'Tis a villain, sir,
I do not love to look on.
Prospero.   But, as 'tis,   310
We cannot miss him; he does make our fire,

Why called dull?—297. **correspondent.** "Used to this day in a religious sense by Catholic writers in reference to grace." *Phila. Shakes. Soc.*—298. **spriting** = work as a spirit?—**gently** = meekly? nobly? willingly, without reluctance [Schmidt]?—**after two days.** Why *two days?* See the last five lines of the play; also line 420.—301. **like a nymph,** etc. Why 'like a nymph of the sea,' if he was to be invisible? That the English *audience*, which Prospero was not thinking of, might see him?—302. Steevens, Dyce, Hudson, and Deighton strike out *thine and.* Wisely?— "Ariel is swayed more by fear than gratitude, a fact which excites Prospero's anger. . . . Prospero is chafed with certain obstacles in the magic sphere of his working, and occasionally wroth with Ariel and Caliban for resistance expressed or implied. He is also liable to perturbation of mind from forgetfulness, as in the Fourth Act, when he suddenly remembers the conspiracy of Caliban. And thus, with all his moral excellence, Prospero is made to awaken our sympathy for a natural imperfection." Heraud's *Shakespeare — His Inner Life,* 1865.

307. **strangeness,** etc. Was that the real cause of her sleeping?—
311. **miss** = to be without [Schmidt]? do without [Wright, Hudson, Rolfe,

SCENE II.] *THE TEMPEST.* 49

Fetch in our wood, and serves in offices
That profit us. — What, ho! slave! Caliban!
Thou earth, thou! speak.
    Caliban. [*Within*]   There's wood enough within.
    Prospero. Come forth, I say! there's other business for thee;
Come, thou tortoise! when? —

    Enter ARIEL, *like a water-nymph.*

Fine apparition! My quaint Ariel,
Hark in thine ear.
    Ariel.   My lord, it shall be done.   [*Exit.*
    Prospero. Thou poisonous slave, come forth!

    Enter CALIBAN.

    Caliban. As wicked dew as e'er my mother brush'd   320
With raven's feather from unwholesome fen
Drop on you both! a south-west blow on ye,
And blister you all o'er?
    Prospero. For this, be sure, to-night thou shalt have cramps,

---

Phillpotts, etc.]? — 316. **tortoise.** Hunter says "there is a good deal that is Hebraistic in this play," and that Caliban "is, as to form, no other than the fish.idol of Ashdod, the Dagon of the Philistines!" Test this, *1 Sam.* v, 4,
    "Dagon his name, sea-monster, upward man
    And downward fish." — *Par. Lost*, I, 462, 463.

Is the treatment of Caliban by Prospero creditable? — **when?** — tience? See in *Jul. Cæs.*, II, i, 5, "When, Lucius, when?" — **quaint.** 'Lat. *cognitus*, known, famous, and *comptus*, neat, adorned; Old Fr. *coint*, defined by Cotgrave, 'quaint, compt, neat, fine, spruce, brisk, smirk, smug, dainty, trim, tricked up.' — See our ed. of *Mer. of Ven.*, II, iv, 6. — "Caliban is malicious, cowardly, false, and base in his inclinations; and yet he is essentially different from the vulgar knaves of a civilized world, as they are occasionally portrayed by Shakespeare. He is rude, but not vulgar; he never falls into the prosaic and low familiarity of his drunken associates, for he is a poetical being in his way; he always speaks in verse." Schlegel's *Lectures on Dram. Literature*, 1815.
    320. **wicked** = baneful? mischievous? sinful? — In *Shakes.* mental and moral qualities are continually imputed to inanimate objects. Is it so here? — 322. **southwest.** ."A noxious character is attributed in *Shakes.* to southerly winds." See *Coriol.*, I, iv, 30; II, iii, 26-30. But why *blister?* Do the commentators seem to forget that this island may have been near the African coast, where the hot winds from the desert sometimes shrivel

Side-stitches that shall pen thy breath up; urchins
Shall, for that vast of night that they may work,
All exercise on thee; thou shalt be pinch'd
As thick as honeycomb, each pinch more stinging
Than bees that made 'em.
 Caliban.   I must eat my dinner.
This island's mine, by Sycorax my mother,   330
Which thou tak'st from me. When thou camest first,
Thou strok'dst me and made much of me, wouldst give me
Water with berries in 't, and teach me how
To name the bigger light, and how the less,
That burn by day and night; and then I lov'd thee,
And show'd thee all the qualities o' the isle,
The fresh springs, brine-pits, barren place and fertile.
Cursed be I that did so! All the charms
Of Sycorax, toads, beetles, bats, light on you!
For I am all the subjects that you have,   340
Which first was mine own king; and here you sty me
In this hard rock, whiles you do keep from me
The rest o' the island.
 Prospero.   Thou most lying slave,
Whom stripes may move, not kindness! I have us'd thee,
Filth as thou art, with human care, and lodg'd thee
In mine own cell, till thou didst seek to violate
The honor of my child.

---

and blister? — 325. **urchins** = fairies [Douce, White]? hedgehogs [Steevens, Jephson]? evil spirits in the form of hedgehogs, mischievous elves [Meiklejohn]? hobgoblins [Wright]? — Lat. *ericius;* Old Fr. *ericon;* Fr. *hérisson;* Early Eng. *irchon;* Mid. Eng. *urchon*, a hedgehog. See *Macbeth*, IV, i, 2. — 326. **that vast of night that they may work** = that empty stretch of night wherein they may work [Wright]? — See F*rness* for a discussion of this passage. — *vast* = waste. — *Hamlet* (see our ed., I, ii, 198) has

'In the dead vast and middle of the night.'

Hudson explains this line in *Hamlet* as meaning 'in the silent void or vacancy of the night, when spirits were anciently supposed to walk abroad.' — 328. **thick.** numerous? full of (pinches) [Deighton]? — **honeycomb** = cells of the honeycomb [Wright]? — 332. **made much.** So the folio. — 333. **water with berries in it** = coffee? — 334. **bigger light,** etc. — *Genesis*, i, 16. — "A special literary panegyric of the blessings of an uncivilized state of society was in existence in one of the *Essays* of Montaigne, translated by Florio in 1603. . . . It seems difficult to escape from the conclusion, that Shakespeare intended his monster as a satire incarnate on Montaigne's 'noble savage.'" Ward's *Hist. of Eng. Dramatic Literature*, 1875.

Caliban.   O ho, O ho! would 't had been done!
Thou didst prevent me; I had peopled else
This isle with Calibans.
   Miranda.   Abhorred slave,
Which any print of goodness wilt not take,   350
Being capable of all ill! I pitied thee,
Took pains to make thee speak, taught thee each hour
One thing or other; when thou didst not, savage,
Know thine own meaning, but wouldst gabble like
A thing most brutish, I endow'd thy purposes
With words that made them known. But thy vile race,
Though thou didst learn, had that in 't which good natures
Could not abide to be with; therefore wast thou
Deservedly confin'd into this rock,
Who hadst deserv'd more than a prison.   360
   Caliban. You taught me language; and my profit on 't
Is, I know how to curse. The red plague rid you
For learning me your language!
   Prospero.   Hag-seed, hence!
Fetch us in fuel; and be quick, thou'rt best,
To answer other business. Shrug'st thou, malice?
If thou neglect'st, or dost unwillingly
What I command, I'll rack thee with old cramps,

---

349. **Abhorred slave,** etc. This speech the folio gives to Miranda. But most of the editors — Theobald, Wright, Hudson, Rolfe, White, Deighton, Phillpotts, etc. — have substituted Prospero as the speaker. With Staunton, Krauth, and Furness, we prefer to follow the folio. Notwithstanding its severity, there is in the speech a feminine delicacy, which strongly contrasts with the masculine coarseness of Prospero. Besides, it is pleasant to think of the little girl as trying to teach the poor brute; while her father teaches *her!* See also II, ii, 128; III, ii, 58. — 359. **into.** See on 277. — 361. **on 't.** See on 87. *Abbott*, 182. — **profit . . . to curse.** Too much of our so-called education finds such issue! — 362. **red plague** = erysipelas [Steevens]? leprosy (*Leviticus*, xiii, 42, 43) [Rolfe, Krauth]? one of three different kinds of plague sores, red, yellow, and black [Halliwell, Hudson, Schmidt]? Might refer to the red crosses on the doors of infected houses in Shakespeare's time [Grey]? — 363. **learning.** Used transitively? So in *Cymbeline*, I, v, 12, and in *Spenser* and the Bible. — 364. **best** = 'best off' (spoken colloquially), in best condition? — 'You were best' (= it were best for you) was the original, and 'you' was properly the dative? Blunderingly the 'you' came to be treated as a nominative in such phrases, and then *I* and *thou* were also used. — *Abbott*, 230. — 367. **old** = abundant [Rolfe, Deighton]? huge (intensive) [Hudson]? what one has known of old, and therefore remarkable or extreme [Meiklejohn]? had of old or aforetime [Furness]? such as the old are subject to [Schmidt]? — See 'aged cramps,' IV, i, 256; also *Macbeth*, II, iii, 2; *Mer. of Ven.*, IV, ii, 15.

Fill all thy bones with aches, make thee roar,
That beasts shall tremble at thy din.
 Caliban.   No, pray thee.
[*Aside*] I must obey; his art is of such power, 370
It would control my dam's god, Setebos,
And make a vassal of him.
 Prospero.   So, slave; hence! [*Exit Caliban.*

Enter FERDINAND, *and* ARIEL (*invisible*) *playing and singing.*

     Ariel's Song.

Come unto these yellow sands,
 And then take hands:
Curtsied when you have, and kiss'd
 The wild waves whist,
Foot it featly here and there;
And, sweet sprites, the burthen bear.
 Hark, Hark!

---

368. **aches.** John Kemble, the actor, made it a dissyllable, and when he personated Prospero, he pronounced it *aitches*. One night, Kemble being ill, Mr. Cook took his place, and the London critics, who were strenuously disputing as to the proper pronunciation, listened eagerly for his utterance. He left the whole line out! The newspapers made him soliloquize as follows: —

  "*Aitches* or *akes*, shall I speak both or either?
  If *akes*, I violate my Shakespeare's measure —
  If *aitches*, I shall give King Johnny pleasure;
  I've hit upon't — by Jove! I'll utter neither!"

See, *post*, III, iii, 2; also *Much Ado*, III, iv, 47-50. — 369. **that.** Line 85. Abbott, 283. — **pray thee.** Very common ellipsis? *Abbott*, 401. Shortened to *prithee.* — 371. "They [the Patagonians] roared like bulls, and cried upon their great devil, Setebos, to help them." Story of Magellan's voyage (in 1519) in Eden's *History of Travaile*, published (1577) when Shakespeare was 13. — Setebos is said by Malone, copying Capell, to be mentioned in Hakluyt's *Voyages* (1598). — 375. **curtsied,** or *courtesied?* — **kiss'd . . . whist** = kissed . . . into silence? — A great deal of ingenuity has been expended on this passage. Perhaps the best interpretation is that of Allen approved by Furness, as follows: "The nymphs are formed on the sands for a dance; the waves . . . are spectators, restless and noisy until the spectacle shall begin . . . When the nymphs indicate, by taking hands, courtesying to and kissing partners, that they *are* beginning, the waves are hushed into silent attention; and thus the nymphs do in *effect* 'kiss the wild waves whist.'" In Milton's *Hymn on the Nativity*, v, 4, *whist* = silenced. — 377. **featly** = skilfully? neatly? — Lat. *factum*, Fr. *fait*, a deed, fr. *facĕre*, to do; Eng. *feat*, a deed well done, an exploit. — 378. **burthen** (Fr. *bourdon*, drone or bass; a *humble-bee;* akin to *burr*, to buzz, an imitative word), a verse repeated in song, a refrain.

Scene II.]   THE TEMPEST.   53

   [*Burthen, dispersedly, within.*   *Bow-wow.*]   380
    The watch-dogs bark.
   [*Burthen, within.*   *Bow-wow.*]
    Hark, Hark! I hear
    The strain of strutting chanticleer
    Cry, Cock a-didle-dow.

Ferdinand. Where should this music be? i' the air or
  the earth? —
It sounds no more; — and, sure, it waits upon
Some god o' the island.   Sitting on a bank,
Weeping again the king my father's wrack,
This music crept by me upon the waters,   390
Allaying both their fury and my passion
With it's sweet air; thence I have follow'd it,
Or it hath drawn me rather.   But 'tis gone. —
No, it begins again.

      Ariel's Song.

  Full fathom five thy father lies;
   Of his bones are coral made;
  Those are pearls that were his eyes:
   Nothing of him that doth fade,
  But doth suffer a sea-change
  Into something rich and strange.   400
  Sea-nymphs hourly ring his knell:
    [*Burthen within.*   *Ding-dong.*]
  Hark! now I hear them — Ding-dong, bell.

Ferdinand.   The ditty does remember my drown'd father.

---

  386. **should.** Used, says Abbott (325), in direct questions about the past where 'shall' was used about the future. — Ferdinand here falls into a reverie [Strachey]? — 389. **again** = again and again [Abbott, 27; Rolfe]? — 391. **passion.** Lat. *passio*, suffering; fr. παθειν, pathein, Lat. *pati*, to suffer. — 392. **it's.** So the folio. See on 95. — 395. **fathom.** A. S. *fædm*, embrace; hence the length of the arms extended to embrace all; six feet. For the 'singular,' see on line 53. Note the alliteration. — 396. **are.** Is 'coral' virtually plural, a sort of 'collective noun'? Or does the proximity of the plural 'bones' control the 'number' of the verb? Or did Shakes. wish to avoid the sound of *bones is?* Abbott, 412. — In *Macbeth*, V, viii, 56, 'pearl' means a circle or group of noblemen. — 397. **pearls.** See on *deck'd*, line 155. — 403. **ding-dong.** See *Mer. of Ven.*, III, ii, 71, 72. Our language is rich in *onomatopœia*, in which Professor Whitney thinks he finds the main originating principle of language. — 404. **remember.** Commemorate? call to (my) mind? recollect? remind of? Note on line 243. —

This is no mortal business, nor no sound
That the earth owes. — I hear it now above me.
 Prospero. The fringed curtains of thine eye advance,
And say what thou seest yond.
 Miranda. What is't? a spirit?
Lord, how it looks about! Believe me, sir,
It carries a brave form. But 'tis a spirit. 410
 Prospero. No, wench; it eats and sleeps and hath such
  senses
As we have — such. This gallant which thou seest
Was in the wrack; and, but he's something stain'd
With grief that's beauty's canker, thou mightst call him
A goodly person. He hath lost his fellows,
And strays about to find 'em.
 Miranda. I might call him
A thing divine, for nothing natural
I ever saw so noble.
 Prospero. [*Aside*] It goes on, I see,
As my soul prompts it. — Spirit, fine spirit! I'll free thee
Within two days for this.

---

405. — **nor no** = nor any? Force of double negative? *Abbott*, 406. In Early E. the desire of emphasis doubtless gave rise to many such. Thus: "No son, were he never so old of years, might not marry." Ascham's *Scholemaster*. — 406. **owes** = possesses? Often so in *Shakes*. Line 453; III, i, 45. See our *Macbeth*, I, iii, 76. — *Abbott*, 290. — 407. **fringed curtains of thine eye advance** = look? open your eyes? Does this sound like Shakespeare diction? — "The solemnity of the phraseology assigned to Prospero is completely in character, recollecting his preternatural capacity." Coleridge's *Seven Lectures*. In Pericles, Thaisa's eyelashes are called 'fringes of bright gold.' In IV, i, 177, we read 'advanc'd their eyelids.' — *Advance* in *Shakes*. often means *lift up*. Lat. *ab*, from; *ante*, before; Fr. *avancer*, to go before. — 408. **yond.** See on II, ii, 20. — A. S. *geon, geond*, there, at a distance; Ger. *jener*. — 412. **gallant.** Late Lat. *galare*, to regale; O. Fr. *galer*, fr. Goth. *gailjan*, to rejoice; Fr. and Ital. *gala*, finery, festivity. *Brachet, Worc*. — 413. **but** = were it not that; but that; except? — *Abbott*, 120. — **something** = a thing? somewhat? in some degree? III, i, 58; *Mer. of Ven.*, I, ii, 124; *Hamlet*, III, i, 173; *Abbott*, 68. — 414. **canker** = rust or tarnish [Hudson, who quotes *James*, v, 3]? canker-worm [Rolfe, Deighton, Schmidt; and Wright, who quotes, "But now will canker sorrow eat my bud," *King John*, III, iv, 82]? — "Shakes. uses 'canker' in four senses; the canker-worm, dog-rose, cancer, and rust." *Hudson*. — 415. Note the antithesis between 'goodly person' and 'thing divine.' — 420. **two days.** I, ii, 298. — "Fouqué would have made Ariel a female spirit becoming Miranda by the power of love, and marriage to Ferdinand; but how much finer, because truer, is Shakespeare's Miranda, a real and complete woman from first to last! Fouqué's conception is indeed very charming, but wants the reality of Shakespeare's, without surpassing it in poetic ideality." *Sir Edward Strachey* in *Quarterly Review*, July, 1890.

Ferdinand. Most sure, the goddess 420
On whom these airs attend! — Vouchsafe my prayer
May know if you remain upon this island;
And that you will some good instruction give
How I may bear me here: my prime request,
Which I do last pronounce, is, O you wonder!
If you be maid or no?
Miranda. No wonder, sir,
But certainly a maid.
Ferdinand. My language! heavens! —
I am the best of them that speak this speech,
Were I but where 'tis spoken.
Prospero. How! the best?
What wert thou, if the King of Naples heard thee? 430
Ferdinand. A single thing, as I am now, that wonders
To hear thee speak of Naples. He does hear me,
And that he does I weep; myself am Naples,
Who with mine eyes, never since at ebb, beheld
The king my father wrack'd.
Miranda. Alack, for mercy!
Ferdinand. Yes, faith, and all his lords; the Duke of Milan
And his brave son being twain.
Prospero. [*Aside*] The Duke of Milan
And his more braver daughter could control thee,

---

420. **sure, the goddess.** Vergil's *O, dea, certe!* O, a goddess, surely! *Æneid*, i, 328; *Comus*, 267. — 421. **vouchsafe.** See our *Jul. Cæs.*, II, i, 313. — The omission of 'that,' which, however, is immediately inserted, shows how plastic the language was in Shakespeare's time. *Abbott*, 285. — 426. **maid** = unmarried? Lines 446-448. — The 1st folio has 'Mayd.' The 4th folio has 'made,' which all the editors down to Singer, 1826, adopted, playing on the word! "Since then, every editor, without exception, I believe, has followed the first folio." *Furness*. — 431. **single** = feeble? unmarried? — "Ferdinand plays upon the word. He believes that himself and the King of Naples are one and the same person; he therefore uses this epithet with a reference to its further sense of *solitary*, and so *feeble and helpless*." *Wright*. See our *Macbeth*, I, iii, 140; vi, 16. White quotes as analogous the phrase 'one-horse town.' — 433. **I am Naples.** Shakes. often gives the king the name of his realm. "*L'état; c'est moi*," I am the state, said the French monarch. See our *Hamlet*, I, i, 61. — 437. **brave son.** Scrutinize the *dramatis personæ*. Might Adrian be he? Fleay suggests that "perhaps Francisco is what is left of him"! Was Shakespeare forgetful? — 438. **more braver.** Line 19. — **control** = confute [Johnson, Schmidt, etc.]? contradict [Wright]? rule? Fuller has, "This report was controlled to be false." — O. Fr. *contre-rôle*, a duplicate register, used to verify the first or official roll. *Brachet*. O. Fr. *contre*,

If now 'twere fit to do't. — At the first sight
They have chang'd eyes. — Delicate Ariel, 440
I'll set thee free for this. — [*To him*] A word, good sir;
I fear you have done yourself some wrong: a word.
　Miranda. Why speaks my father so ungently? This
Is the third man that e'er I saw, the first
That e'er I sigh'd for; pity move my father
To be inclin'd my way!
　Ferdinand.　　　　O, if a virgin,
And your affection not gone forth, I'll make you
The Queen of Naples.
　Prospero.　　　　Soft, sir! one word more. —
[*Aside*] They are both in either's powers; but this swift business
I must uneasy make, lest too light winning 450
Make the prize light. — [*To him*] One word more; I charge thee
That thou attend me. Thou dost here usurp
The name thou owest not, and hast put thyself
Upon this island as a spy, to win it
From me, the lord on't.
　Ferdinand.　　　　No, as I am a man.
　Miranda. There's nothing ill can dwell in such a temple;
If the ill spirit have so fair a house,
Good things will strive to dwell with't.
　Prospero. [*To Ferdinand*]　　　　Follow me. —
Speak not you for him; he's a traitor. — Come;
I'll manacle thy neck and feet together: 460
Sea-water shalt thou drink; thy food shall be

Lat. *contra*, over against; *rôle*, Lat. *rotŭlus*, a roll. — 440. **changed eyes.** "It is love at first sight, and it appears to me that in all cases of real love, it is at one moment that it takes place." *Coleridge.* — 442. **wrong.** What? — A polite way of saying 'You are mistaken,' or something plainer still [Wright]? — 443. **Why speaks,** etc. Answered in 449–451? — 445. **pity move.** *Abbott*, 364, 365. — 446. — O, if, etc. Line 426. *Abbott*, 387. — 448. **soft** = hold? stop? *Mer. of Ven.*, IV, i, 312. — 449. In Shakespeare's 28th sonnet, we have, 'And each, though enemies to either's reign'; in *Henry V*, II, ii, 106, 'As two yoke-devils sworn to either's purpose.' — *Abbott*, 12. — 452. **attend** = wait on, or follow? accompany? attend to? *Abbott*, 200, 369. Ellipsis? — 453. **owest** = dost possess? ownest? art indebted to? See on 405. — 456. **temple.** Is this a trace of Shakespeare's Bible reading? *1 Corinth.*, vi, 19; *2 Corinth.*, vi, 16; *Macbeth*, II, iii, 49. — 460. **manacle,** etc. Neck and feet were drawn close together, and the position soon became one of terrible torture. — Lat. *manus*, hand, from MA, Sansk. *mâ*, to measure; Lat. *manica*, a long sleeve, glove, gauntlet,

The fresh-brook muscles, wither'd roots, and husks
Wherein the acorn cradled.   Follow.
Ferdinand.   No;
I will resist such entertainment till
Mine enemy has more power.
                    [*He draws, and is charmed from moving.*
Miranda.   O dear father!
Make not too rash a trial of him, for
He's gentle, and not fearful.
    Prospero.   What! I say,
My foot my tutor?—Put thy sword up, traitor,
Who mak'st a show, but dar'st not strike, thy conscience
Is so possess'd with guilt: come from thy ward;   470
For I can here disarm thee with this stick,
And make thy weapon drop.
    Miranda.   Beseech you, father!
    Prospero. Hence! hang not on my garments.
    Miranda.   Sir, have pity;
I'll be his surety.
    Prospero.   Silence! one word more
Shall make me chide thee, if not hate thee!   What!
An advocate for an impostor! hush!
Thou think'st there is no more such shapes as he,
Having seen but him and Caliban; foolish wench!
To the most of men this is a Caliban,
And they to him are angels.
    Miranda.   My affections   480
Are, then, most humble; I have no ambition
To see a goodlier man.

---

handcuff; *manicula*, dimin.—467. **gentle** = 'of gentle blood,' high-born [Wright, Rolfe, Phillpotts]? noble, high-minded, of a lofty spirit [Smollett, Staunton, Hudson]? kind [Schmidt]? mild and harmless [Ritson, Furness]?—**fearful** = timid, cowardly [Warburton, Holt, Smollett, Staunton]? formidable, terrible [Malone, Ritson, Wright, Deighton, Furness]? "There may be a covert play upon the other significations both of 'gentle' and 'fearful.'" *Wright.*—468.—**my foot my tutor?** Similar expressions are repeatedly found in authors of the Elizabethan age. Yet Walker proposed and Dyce and Hudson adopted *fool* for foot!—'The foot above the head.' *Timon of Ath.*, I, i, 95, 96.—470. **ward** = 'guard' made in fencing, posture of defence [Schmidt]? Says Falstaff (*1 Henry IV*, II, iv, 181, 182), "Thou knowest my old *ward*; here I lay, and thus I bore my point. Four rogues in buckram let drive at me."—Teut. base WAR, to defend; A. S. *weard*, guard, watchman. *Guard* is a doublet of *ward*.— 472. **beseech you.** Ellipsis? Line 369. The desire of brevity a sufficient explanation? *Abbott*, 283.—477. **there is.** See on 'cares,' I, i, 16,

Prospero. [*To Ferdinand*] Come on; obey:
Thy nerves are in their infancy again,
And have no vigor in them.
    Ferdinand.   So they are;
My spirits, as in a dream, are all bound up.
My father's loss, the weakness which I feel,
The wrack of all my friends, nor this man's threats
To whom I am subdued, are but light to me,
Might I but through my prison once a day
Behold this maid. All corners else o' the earth   490
Let liberty make use of; space enough
Have I in such a prison.
    Prospero. [*Aside*] It works. — [*To Ferdinand*] Come on. —
Thou hast done well, fine Ariel! — Follow me. —
[*To Ariel*] Hark what thou else shalt do me.
    Miranda.   Be of comfort.
My father's of a better nature, sir,
Than he appears by speech; this is unwonted
Which now came from him.
    Prospero.   Thou shalt be as free
As mountain winds; but then exactly do
All points of my command.
    Ariel.   To the syllable.
    Prospero. Come, follow. — Speak not for him.   [*Exeunt.*

—483. **nerves.** Cotgrave (1632) defines *nerf* thus: 'a synnow [sinew]; and thence might, strength, force, power.' Schmidt says that, in *Shakes.*, 'nerve' is 'that in which the strength of a body lies,' and that it rather is equivalent to 'sinew, tendon, than an organ of sensation and motion.' — *Hamlet*, I, iv, 83. — In Milton's *Comus*, 659, 660, we have

"Nay, lady, sit: if I but wave this wand,
  Your nerves are all chained up in alabaster."

485. **as in a dream.** *Æneid*, xii, 908–912. — 487. **nor.** Supply the ellipsis. *Abbott*, 396. — 488. **but** = otherwise than? merely? — 489. **might I,** etc. So in Chaucer's *Knight's Tale*, 370–380 (1228–1237, Gilman's ed., 1879). So Lovelace (1618–1658) sings in prison, —

"When Love with unconfined wings
  Hovers within my gates,
And my divine Althea brings
  To whisper at my grates.
    . . . .

Stone walls do not a prison make,
  Nor iron bars a cage;
Minds innocent and quiet take
  That for a hermitage.

If I have freedom in my love,
  And in my soul am free,
Angels alone that soar above
  Enjoy such liberty."

ACT II.

Scene I. *Another Part of the Island.*

Enter Alonso, Sebastian, Antonio, Gonzalo, Adrian Francisco, *and others.*

Gonzalo. Beseech you, sir, be merry; you have cause —
So have we all — of joy; for our escape
Is much beyond our loss. Our hint of woe
Is common: every day, some sailor's wife,
The masters of some merchant, and the merchant,
Have just our theme of woe; but for the miracle —
I mean our preservation — few in millions
Can speak like us: then wisely, good sir, weigh
Our sorrow with our comfort.
 Alonso.   Prithee, peace.
 Sebastian. He receives comfort like cold porridge.   10
 Antonio. The visitor will not give him o'er so.
 Sebastian. Look, he's winding up the watch of his wit; by and by it will strike.
 Gonzalo. Sir, —
 Sebastian. One; tell.

Act II. Scene I. Lines 1, 2. Keightley transposes thus:

> "You have cause
> Of joy, — so have we all."

He declares the original text a 'printer's error.' But Gonzalo wishes to emphasize *joy*. By holding it back, does it not come out later with more emphasis? — 3. **hint.** I, ii, 134. — 5. **merchant** = merchantman? trading vessel? So in Marlowe's *Tamburlaine*, —

> "And Christian merchants, that, with Russian stems
> Plough up huge furrows in the Caspian seas."

— 11. **visitor.** Peculiar sense? — "I was sick, and ye visited me." *Matt.*, xxv, 36. — 12. **winding . . . watch.** "The invention of striking watches is ascribed to Peter Hele, of Nuremberg, about the year 1510." *W. A. Wright.* — 15. **tell.** A. S. *tellan*, to count. So 'tellers' count money or votes; 'all told,' 'tell off,' 'untold wealth,' etc.; *Psalms*, xlviii,

Gonzalo. When every grief is entertain'd that's offer'd,
Comes to the entertainer —
Sebastian. A dollar.
Gonzalo. Dolor comes to him, indeed; you have spoken truer than you purpos'd. 20
Sebastian. You have taken it wiselier than I meant you should.
Gonzalo. 'Therefore, my lord, —
Antonio. Fie, what a spendthrift is he of his tongue!
Alonso. I prithee, spare.
Gonzalo. Well, I have done; but yet, —
Sebastian. He will be talking.
Antonio. Which — of — he or Adrian — for a good wager, first begins to crow?
Sebastian. The old cock. 30
Antonio. The cockerel.
Sebastian. Done. The wager?
Antonio. A laughter.
Sebastian. A match!
Adrian. Though this island seem to be desert, —
Antonio. Ha, ha, ha!
Sebastian. So, you're paid.
Adrian. Uninhabitable, and almost inaccessible, —
Sebastian. Yet, —
Adrian. Yet, — 40
Antonio. He could not miss't.
Adrian. It must needs be of subtle, tender, and delicate temperance.
Antonio. Temperance was a delicate wench.
Sebastian. Ay, and a subtle; as he most learnedly deliver'd. 46
Adrian. The air breathes upon us here most sweetly.
Sebastian. As if it had lungs, and rotten ones.

---

12. — 18, 19, **dollar** . . . **dolor.** The paronomasia is ancient. *Lear*, II, iv, 50. — 28. **of he or Adrian.** Justify 'he.' Suppose Antonio begins 'Which of,' and then checks himself, saying (or implying by a gesture, 'is it') '*he?* or *Adrian?*' In an undertone? — 'Like the French Lequel preferez-vous de Corneille ou de Racine.' Phila. *Sh. Soc.* — *Abbott*, 206, '*he* for *him*'; *Furness*, on *As You L. I.*, III, ii, (337) 356. — Note in V, i, 15, '**him**' for '**he**.' — 31. **cockerel.** Said to be a double dimin., like *pick-er-el*, *mack-er-el*. — 36. Which won? — 37. **paid.** Explain. — 43. **temperance** = temperature [Steevens]? — 44. **was.** Emphatic? The virtues **made** convenient names? — 45. **deliver'd** = related? declared?

Antonio. Or as 'twere perfumed by a fen.
Gonzalo. Here is every thing advantageous to life. 50
Antonio. True; save means to live.
Sebastian. Of that there's none, or little.
Gonzalo. How lush and lusty the grass looks! how green!
Antonio. The ground, indeed, is tawny.
Sebastian. With an eye of green in't.
Antonio. He misses not much.
Sebastian. No; he doth but mistake the truth totally.
Gonzalo. But the rarity of it is, — which is indeed almost beyond credit, —
Sebastian. As many vouched rarities are. 60
Gonzalo. That our garments, being, as they were, drenched in the sea, hold, notwithstanding, their freshness and glosses being rather new-dyed than stained with salt water.
Antonio. If but one of his pockets could speak, would it not say he lies?
Sebastian. Ay, or very falsely pocket up his report.
Gonzalo. Methinks our garments are now as fresh as when we put them on first in Afric, at the marriage of the king's fair daughter Claribel to the King of Tunis.
Sebastian. 'Twas a sweet marriage, and we prosper well in our return. 71
Adrian. Tunis was never graced before with such a paragon to their queen.

---

formally uttered speech-fashion? — 48, 49. *Coriolanus*, III, iii, 120, 121. — 53. **lush and lusty.** "Shakes. has 'lush' (short for luscious) in the sense of luxuriant in growth, where Chaucer would certainly have said *lusty*; the curious result being that Shakes. uses both words together." *Skeat*. See Tennyson's *Dream of Fair Women*, line 71. — 54. **tawny.** Another spelling of *tanny*, i.e. resembling that which is tanned by the sun. *Skeat*. See on *orange-tawny* in our *Mid. N. Dr.*, I, ii, 82. — 55. **eye of green.** Is 'eye' put for what the eye reveals? — eye = small shade [Steevens]? small portion [Malone]? quibbling reference to green-eyed credulity [Hunter]? — "The jesting pair mean that the grass is really tawny (*tanned, dried up*), and that the only 'green' spot in it is Gonzalo himself." *Phillpotts.* — 63. **stained**, etc. "Sea-water freshens and cleanses woollen cloth." Stearns's *Shakespeare Treasury.* — 64. **pockets**, etc. Supposed full of mud? — 65. **pocket-up** = conceal (as in the pocket)? pusillanimously ignore? take clandestinely or fraudulently? — 72. **paragon.** *Hamlet*, II, ii, 302. — Span. *para* (from Lat. *pro*, forth, and *ad*, to), in comparison; *con*, Lat. *cum*, with; Fr. and Span. *paragon*, pattern, perfect model. *Skeat*. Webster's *Int. Dict.* makes it fr. Gr. παρά, para, beside, and ἀκόνη, akone, whetstone. — 73. **to.** So "Wilt thou have this woman to thy wedded wife," in the 'Marriage Office' in the *Book of Common Prayer*; *Mark*, xii, 23. See III, iii, 54; *Abbott*, 189. —

Gonzalo. Not since widow Dido's time.

Antonio. Widow! a plague o' that! How came that widow in? Widow Dido!

Sebastian. What if he had said widower Æneas too? Good Lord, how you take it!

Adrian. Widow Dido, said you? you make me study of that; she was of Carthage, not of Tunis. 80

Gonzalo. This Tunis, sir, was Carthage.

Adrian. Carthage?

Gonzalo. I assure you, Carthage.

Antonio. His word is more than the miraculous harp.

Sebastian. He hath raised the wall, and houses too.

Antonio. What impossible matter will he make easy next?

Sebastian. I think he will carry this island home in his pocket, and give it his son for an apple.

Antonio. And, sowing the kernels of it in the sea, bring forth more islands. 90

Gonzalo. Ay?

Antonio. Why, in good time.

Gonzalo. Sir, we were talking that our garments seem now as fresh as when we were at Tunis at the marriage of your daughter, who is now queen.

Antonio. And the rarest that e'er came there.

Sebastian. Bate, I beseech you, widow Dido.

Antonio. O, widow Dido! ay, widow Dido.

Gonzalo. Is not, sir, my doublet as fresh as the first day I wore it? I mean, in a sort. 100

Antonio. That sort was well fished for.

Gonzalo. When I wore it at your daughter's marriage?

---

74. **Dido.** Troy is said to have been captured about 1184 B.C.; Dido, to have founded Carthage about 853 B.C. Her husband was Sychæus; Æneas' wife, Creusa. It would seem, therefore, that about 330 years intervened between widow and widower; but Vergil cares no more than Shakespeare for accurate chronology. *Æneid*, ii, iv. — 75. **widow.** Ominous! — 80. **Tunis.** Some three or four miles from the ruins of Carthage. — 84. **harp.** Amphion's lyre is said to have raised the walls of Thebes; Apollo's, those of Troy. Has Gonzalo's word made two cities one? — 97. **Bate** = except? omit? See I, ii, 250; also on 'bated' in our *Mer. of Ven.*, I, iii, 114. — 101. **sort** = word 'sort'? Was the word 'fished' suggested by 'sort'? "When the net is drawn, the fish are always, what they term '*sorted*'; some are thrown back into the water, others carried sorted to market." *Dirrill.* See on *association of ideas* our *As You Like It*, II, vii, 44; Furness' Var. Ed. of *As You Like It*, pp. 109-111. —

Alonso.   You cram these words into mine ears against
The stomach of my sense.   Would I had never
Married my daughter there! for, coming thence,
My son is lost; and, in my rate, she too,
Who is so far from Italy remov'd
I ne'er again shall see her.   O thou mine heir
Of Naples and of Milan, what strange fish
Hath made his meal on thee?
   Francisco.   Sir, he may live   110
I saw him beat the surges under him,
And ride upon their backs; he trod the water,
Whose enmity he flung aside, and breasted
The surge most swoln that met him; his bold head
'Bove the contentious waves he kept, and oar'd
Himself with his good arms in lusty stroke
To the shore, that o'er his wave-worn basis bow'd,
As stooping to relieve him.   I not doubt
He came alive to land.
   Alonso.   No, no, he's gone.
   Sebastian.   Sir, you may thank yourself for this great loss,
That would not bless our Europe with your daughter,   121
But rather lose her to an African;
Where she at least is banish'd from your eye,
Who hath cause to wet the grief on't.
   Alonso.   Prithee, peace.
   Sebastian.   You were kneel'd to, and importun'd otherwise,
By all of us; and the fair soul herself
Weigh'd between loathness and obedience, at
Which end o' the beam should bow.   We have lost your son,

---

103. **cram.**   As unpalatable food into one's mouth? — 106. **rate.**   Lat. *reor, ratum*, reckon, think, value, estimate?   I, ii, 92; *Mer. of Ven.*, II, vii, 26. — 113. **enmity.**   Note the vivid personifications in this speech.   *Jul. Cæs.*, I, ii, 104, 105. — 115. **oar'd.**   Observe the turning of other 'parts of speech' into verbs.   *Abbott*, 290. — See *Odyssey*, xii, 444, "I rowed with my hands"; *Par. Lost*, vii, 438. — 117. **his.**   I, ii, 95, 392; *Abbott*, 228; "If the salt have lost his savor," *Matt.*, v, 13. — 118. **not doubt,** V, i, 38, 113, 304; *Abbott*, 305. — 121. **who hath cause,** etc. = who, lost to sight by banishment, though not by death, hath yet cause to fill your eyes with tears [Wright]? which [eye] has cause to give tearful expression to the sorrow for your folly [Abbott, 264]? whose unsuitable marriage might well make you weep [Phillpotts]? which hath cause to sprinkle your grief with tears [Hudson, Meiklejohn, Deighton, etc.]? — 125. **importun'd.**   Accent?   So usually in *Shakes.* — 127. **weigh'd** = was evenly balanced [Wright, Meiklejohn]? hesitated [Hudson]? pondered, deliberated [Furness, Deighton]? — 128. **at which end o' th' beame should bow.**

I fear, forever; Milan and Naples have
Moe widows in them of this business' making, 130
Than we bring men to comfort them: the fault's
Your own.
    Alonso. So is the dear'st o' the loss.
    Gonzalo.   My lord Sebastian,
The truth you speak doth lack some gentleness,
And time to speak it in; you rub the sore,
When you should bring the plaster.
    Sebastian.   Very well.
    Antonio. And most chirurgeonly.
    Gonzalo. It is foul weather in us all, good sir,
When you are cloudy.
    Sebastian.   Foul weather?
    Antonio.   Very foul.
    Gonzalo. Had I plantation of this isle, my lord,— 140
    Antonio. He'd sow 't with nettle-seed.
    Sebastian.   Or docks, or mallows.
    Gonzalo. And were the king on 't, what would I do?
    Sebastian. Scape being drunk, for want of wine.
    Gonzalo. I' the commonwealth I would by contraries
Execute all things; for no kind of traffic
Would I admit; no name of magistrate;

So the folio. But most critics change *should* to 'sh 'ould' or 'she 'd,' meaning *she would*. But they don't tell us why she should make a bow at either end!—The question which she 'weighed,' or at which she hesitated, was, "Shall my 'loathness' (unwillingness, reluctance, disgust) outweigh my duty of obedience to my father, or shall the obedience outweigh the loathness?" In one scale, loathness; in the other, obedience—which end of the beam shall sink? not at which end of the beam shall I bow my head or bend my body!—All the emendations remind us of blacksmiths tinkering watches. See on I, ii, 155.—Personification here, as in lines 117, 118?—130. **moe** is plural. Anciently moe was used of *numbers; more,* of size. *Skeat.*—132. **dear'st.** Often in Shakes. *dear* = heart-touching, as *dearest foe* in *Hamlet,* I, ii, 182. See our ed. For a discussion of the word, see Furness' Var. Ed., *Rom. and Jul.,* V, iii, 32, pp. 272, 273.—136. **chirurgeonly.** Gr. χειρ, cheir, hand; ἔργειν, ergein, work. A 'chirurgeon' (shortened to *surgeon*) is a *hand-worker,* not a drug-giver! Does Shakes. recognize the etymology in "I am indeed, sir, a surgeon to old shoes. . . . As proper men as ever trod upon neat's leather have gone upon my *handiwork.*" Our *Jul. Cæs.,* I, i, 24, 26.—139. **cloudy.** With anger, or sorrow?—140. **plantation** = planting? colonizing.—143. **drunk,** etc. "Shakes. never puts habitual scorn into the mouths of other than bad men," says Coleridge.—145-161. This passage, Capell (1766) and all subsequent commentators declare to be taken from Florio's (1603 or 1604) translation of Montaigne's *Essays.* But whoever would translate *Montaigne* into English must use substan-

Letters should not be known; riches, poverty,
And use of service, none; contract, succession,
Bourn, bound of land, tilth, vineyard, none;
No use of metal, corn, or wine, or oil; 150
No occupation; all men idle, all;
And women too, but innocent and pure;
No sovereignty;—
 Sebastian. Yet he would be king on 't.
 Antonio. The latter end of his commonwealth forgets the beginning.
 Gonzalo. All things in common nature should produce
Without sweat or endeavor: treason, felony,
Sword, pike, knife, gun, or need of any engine,
Would I not have; but nature should bring forth,
Of it own kind, all foison, all abundance 160
To feed my innocent people.
 Sebastian. No marrying 'mong his subjects?
 Antonio. None, man; all idle;—and knaves.
 Gonzalo. I would with such perfection govern, sir,
To excel the golden age.
 Sebastian. Save his majesty!
 Antonio. Long live Gonzalo!
 Gonzalo. And,— do you mark me, sir?—
 Alonso. Prithee, no more; thou dost talk nothing to me.
 Gonzalo. I do well believe your highness; and did it to minister occasion to these gentlemen, who are of such sensible and nimble lungs that they always use to laugh at nothing. 171
 Antonio. 'Twas you we laughed at.

---

tially the same phraseology, and Shakes. may have drawn directly from the French. There is, however, in the British Museum a copy of Florio's translation containing what is supposed to be a genuine autograph of Shakespeare. — 149. **bourn.** 'Doublet' of *bound;* Old Fr. *bonne;* Mod. Fr. *borne,* limit, boundary, landmark. *Brachet, Skeat.*— **tilth.** A. S. *tilian,* to till. The suffix *th* usually denotes condition or state, or the action of a verb taken abstractly. See on *wealth* in our *Mer. of Ven.*, V, i, 237. — 158. **engine** = instrument of war, or military machine [Steevens]? — Lat. *ingenium,* ingenious contrivance. — 160. **It.** See on *it's*, I, ii, 95. — **foison.** Lat. *fusio,* pouring, profusion, IV, i, 110; see our *Macbeth,* IV, iii, 88. — 163. **all idle; whores and knaves.** Cause and effect. — 165. **to** = as to? *Abbott,* 281.— **golden age.** The imagined age of primeval simplicity, purity, and peace. The poets of many nations have sung of such an Eden in the far past. — 169. **sensible** = sensitive? Often so in *Shakes.* — **nimble.** A. S. *niman,* to take. "The sense is 'quick at seizing,' hence active." *Skeat.* Sensitive and nimble lungs are those

Gonzalo. Who, in this kind of merry fooling, am nothing to you; so you may continue, and laugh at nothing still.
Antonio. What a blow was there given!
Sebastian. An it had not fallen flat-long.
Gonzalo. You are gentlemen of brave mettle; you would lift the moon out of her sphere, if she would continue in it five weeks without changing.

Enter ARIEL *(invisible) playing solemn music.*

Sebastian. We would so, and then go a bat-fowling.   180
Antonio. Nay, good my lord, be not angry.
Gonzalo. No, I warrant you; I will not adventure my discretion so weakly. Will you laugh me asleep, for I am very heavy?
Antonio. Go sleep and hear us.
       [*All sleep except Alonso, Sebastian, and Antonio.*
Alonso. What, all so soon asleep! I wish mine eyes Would, with themselves, shut up my thoughts; I find They are inclin'd to do so.
Sebastian.   Please you, sir,
Do not omit the heavy offer of it:
It seldom visits sorrow; when it doth,   190
It is a comforter.
Antonio.   We two, my lord,

---

characterized as 'tickle o' the sere.' *Hamlet*, II, ii, 317.—176. **An** = if? yes, if? *Abbott*, 101.—**flat-long** = striking with the flat side instead of the sharp edge?—Adv. like headlong. Old Eng. dative fem. sing. Morris' *Eng. Accidence*, sec. 311.—So *flatling* in *Faerie Q.*, V, v, 18.—177. **mettle.** Spelled 'mettal' in the folio. So we say 'man of iron,' 'of true steel,' etc.—178. **sphere.** One of the 8 revolving, transparent, hollow, concentric, bubble-like shells of the Ptolemaic or Alphonsine astronomy. In the first 7, the 'seven planets,' i.e. Moon, Mercury, Venus, Sun, Mars, Jupiter, Saturn, respectively, were supposed to be fastened, and in the 8th the fixed stars. *Hamlet*, IV, vii, 15; *Mid. N. Dr.*, II, i, 150; Milton's *Hymn on the Nativity*, stanza xiii.
180. **a bat-fowling.** An ancient mode of catching many sorts of birds in a dark night by blinding or bewildering them with bright torches, having beaten them from their haunts or nests with poles. Markham's *Hunger's Prevention*, 1621, quoted by Furness. The *a* is fr. A. S. *on* or *an*. *Abbott*, 140. See on *amain*, IV, i, 74.—182. **adventure . . . weakly,** etc. = risk so foolishly my reputation for discretion? *Cymbeline*, I, vi, 172.—184. **heavy.** 'Heavy with sleep,' *Luke*, ix, 33. Often for 'drowsy' in *Shakespeare*; oftener for sad, sorrowful. *Mer. of Ven.*, V, i, 130.—185. **hear us.** Keightley and Hudson add 'not' after 'us.' But why not let Antonio have his little jest?—189. **omit.** I, ii, 183. "'Heavy' in this line is proleptic or anticipatory," say the critics.—190. **visits sorrow.** See in Young's *Night Thoughts* the fine lines beginning, 'Tired

Will guard your person while you take your rest,
And watch your safety.
Alonso.   Thank you. — Wondrous heavy.
                             [*Alonso sleeps. Exit Ariel.*
Sebastian. What a strange drowsiness possesses them!
Antonio. It is the quality o' the climate.
Sebastian.   Why
Doth it not then our eyelids sink? I find not
Myself dispos'd to sleep.
   Antonio.   Nor I; my spirits are nimble.
They fell together all, as by consent;
They dropp'd, as by a thunder-stroke. What might,
Worthy Sebastian? — O, what might? — No more. —   200
And yet methinks I see it in thy face,
What thou shouldst be; the occasion speaks thee, and
My strong imagination sees a crown
Dropping upon thy head.
   Sebastian.   What, art thou waking?
Antonio. Do you not hear me speak?
Sebastian.   I do; and surely
It is a sleepy language, and thou speak'st
Out of thy sleep. What is it thou didst say?
This is a strange repose, to be asleep
With eyes wide open; standing, speaking, moving,
And yet so fast asleep.
   Antonio.   Noble Sebastian,   210
Thou let'st thy fortune sleep — die, rather; wink'st
Whiles thou art waking.
   Sebastian.   Thou dost snore distinctly;
There's meaning in thy snores.
   Antonio. I am more serious than my custom: you
Must be so too, if heed me; which to do,
Trebles thee o'er.

---

nature's sweet restorer, balmy sleep.' — **198. consent.** Lat. *consentire*, to agree. Lat. *con*, together; *sentire*, to perceive by the senses, to feel. — **202. shouldst** = oughtest to [Furness]? *Macbeth*, I, iii, 45; *Mer. of Ven.*, II, vi, 44; *Abbott*, 323. — **occasion** = Gr. καιρός, kairos; Lat. *occasio*, critical or favorable moment [Phila. *Shakes. Soc.*]? — **speaks thee** = expresses thee (i.e. shows thee as what thou canst be and what in *posse* thou art now) [Delius]? shows what you are intended for [Jephson]? proclaims thee [Wright]? reveals or proclaims thee [Hudson]? — *Macbeth*, IV, iii, 159; *Henry VIII*, II, iv, 139. — **211. wink'st** = shuttest thine eyes? Line 280; *Acts*, xvii, 30. — **215. if heed.** So 'O, if a virgin,' I, ii, 496. For ellipses in *Shakes.*, see *Abbott*, 382–405. — **216. trebles.** How multi-

Sebastian. Well, I am standing water.
Antonio. I'll teach you how to flow.
Sebastian. Do so; to ebb
Hereditary sloth instructs me.
Antonio. O,
If you but knew how you the purpose cherish
Whiles thus you mock it! how, in stripping it, 220
You more invest it! Ebbing men, indeed,
Most often do so near the bottom run
By their own fear or sloth.
Sebastian. Prithee, say on;
The setting of thine eye and cheek proclaim
A matter from thee, and a birth, indeed,
Which throes thee much to yield.
Antonio. Thus, sir:
Although this lord of weak remembrance, — this,
Who shall be of as little memory
When he is earth'd, — hath here almost persuaded, —
For he's a spirit of persuasion, only 230
Professes to persuade, — the king his son's alive,
'Tis as impossible that he's undrown'd
As he that sleeps here swims.
Sebastian. I have no hope
That he's undrown'd.
Antonio. O, out of that no hope

---

plies by three? *Mer. of Ven.*, III, ii, 153. — Wilson would change *trebles* to 'rebels,' and then interpret 'rebels' as meaning 'ripples,' in which he would find a pun that might suggest 'standing water'! Some 'fooling' is 'admirable,' and some is not. — 218-221. **O, if you knew how . . . invest it**, etc. = O, if you knew how that metaphor, which you use in jest, encourages! how, in stripping off the ambiguous rhetorical dress, you the more clothe the purpose with the garb of reasonableness! Or, if you knew how, "in stripping the words of their common meaning, and using them figuratively, you adapt them to your situation!" The latter explanation was given in the *Edinburgh Magazine*, in Nov., 1786. "The more Sebastian, by putting forward his natural indolence, seems to decline entering into Antonio's counsels, the more, as Antonio can perceive, he is really inclined to slip into them as into a garment" [Phillpotts]? — 226. **throes.** A. S. *threaw*, a pain; *throwian*, to suffer pain; *threowan*, to afflict. — 227. **this lord** = Gonzalo [Johnson, Jephson, Phillpotts, Furness]? Francisco [Capell, Hunter, Hudson]? See 110-119. — Francisco's age? — **of weak remembrance** = remembering little? having a weak memory? — 228. **of as little memory** = as little remembered? — 230. **he's** = he is [Johnson, Furness]? he has [Steevens, Monck Mason, Capell, Dyce, Hunter, Hudson]? — **only professes** = is the only one that professes, or makes a show of (persuading) [Johnson]? his only profession

What great hope have you! no hope that way is
Another way so high a hope that even
Ambition cannot pierce a wink beyond,
But doubt discovery there. Will you grant with me
That Ferdinand is drown'd?
   Sebastian.   He's gone.
   Antonio.   Then, tell me,
Who's the next heir of Naples?
   Sebastian.   Claribel.   240
   Antonio. She that is Queen of Tunis; she that dwells
Ten leagues beyond man's life; she that from Naples
Can have no note, unless the sun were post, —
The man i' the moon's too slow, — till new-born chins
Be rough and razorable; she that from whom
We all were sea-swallow'd, though some cast again,
And by that destiny to perform an act
Whereof what's past is prologue, what to come
In yours and my discharge.
   Sebastian.   What stuff is this! How say you?
'Tis true, my brother's daughter's Queen of Tunis;   250
So is she heir of Naples; 'twixt which regions
There is some space.
   Antonio.   A space whose every cubit
Seems to cry out, 'How shall that Claribel

---

is [Wright, Furness, Meiklejohn]? — 237. Wright suggests the appropriateness of 'wink' in connection with ambition's piercing eye. — 238. **but doubt**, etc. = (cannot) but doubt? cannot pierce beyond without doubting [Phila. *Shakes. Soc.*; Furness, with misgivings]? Many emendations have been proposed. We follow the folio.

242. **man's life** = where men live [Meiklejohn]? a lifetime of travelling [Steevens, Hudson, etc.]? the city Zoa (life) south of Tunis [Hunter]? seventy years [Croft, in *Annotations on Plays of Shakespeare*, 1810]? Croft takes seventy *years*, the Scriptural limit of man's life (*Psalms*, xc, 10), adds ten *leagues* to the seventy *years*, and finds the sum total to be eighty *leagues!* As magnitude of distance is important, why did not Croft reduce the leagues to *miles*, and then say 70 years + 30 miles = 100 miles? — 243. **note** = information, knowledge, intimation [Wright, Hudson, etc.]? letter? — *Mer. of Ven.*, III, iv, 51. — **post** = letter-carrier [Meiklejohn]? *Post* is used more than twenty times for messenger in *Shakes.* — 244. **too slow.** Because lagging behind the sun, losing nearly an hour a day? — 245. **that.** So the folio. Most editors follow Rowe in omitting 'that.' Such apparent anacoluthon, or confusion of constructions, due, perhaps, to ellipsis, is quite natural, and betrays Antonio's excitement? — 246. **cast.** Antithesis of 'swallowed'? Notice how this theatrical word 'cast' (to assign parts to actors) suggests 'act,' 'perform,' 'prologue,' 'discharge.' *Mid. N. Dr.*, I, ii, 83; IV, ii, 8. — 249. **What stuff is this?** A very proper question!

Measure us back to Naples? Keep in Tunis,
And let Sebastian wake.' Say, this were death
That now hath seiz'd them; why, they were no worse
Than now they are. There be that can rule Naples
As well as he that sleeps; lords that can prate
As amply and unnecessarily
As this Gonzalo: I myself could make   260
A chough of as deep chat. O, that you bore
The mind that I do! what a sleep were this
For your advancement! Do you understand me?
  Sebastian. Methinks I do.
  Antonio.   And how does your content
Tender your own good fortune?
  Sebastian.   I remember
You did supplant your brother Prospero.
  Antonio.   True:
And look how well my garments sit upon me;
Much feater than before. My brother's servants
Were then my fellows, now they are my men.
  Sebastian. But, for your conscience —   270
  Antonio. Ay, sir; where lies that? If 'twere a kibe,
'Twould put me to my slipper; but I feel not
This deity in my bosom. Twenty consciences,
That stand 'twixt me and Milan, candied be they,
And melt, ere they molest! Here lies your brother,
No better than the earth he lies upon,
If he were that which now he's like, — that's dead;
Whom I, with this obedient steel, three inches of it,

---

253. **us** = us cubits? — Hudson changes 'shall that' to 'shalt thou.' — **keep** = keep she? let her keep? — Keep is still used for 'live,' or 'stay,' 'dwell,' in portions of New England. — 257. **be**; plural, shortened from E. E. *been*? III, i, 1. — 261. **make** = become? create? train to be? — **make a chough . . . chat** = train a chough to talk as deeply [Jephson]? — *chough*, a red-legged Cornish crow. — *All's Well*, IV, i, 18.

264. **content** = contentment, apathy [Hudson, Deighton]? favorable judgment [Rolfe]? — 265. **tender** = take care of, look out for [Hudson]? esteem [Phillpotts]? regard [Rolfe, Meiklejohn]? or value [Rolfe]? *Henry V*, II, ii, 175; *As You Like It*, V, ii, 65. — 268. **feater**. See on I, ii, 377. — 271. **kibe** = chilblain? chap in the heel? sore heel? — See note in our *Hamlet*, V, i, 134. — 273. **deity**. Sarcastic? — Scan. *Abbott*, 471. — 274. **candied** = congealed. [Malone, Schmidt, Hudson, Rolfe, Deighton, Meiklejohn]? sugared over, and so insensible [Wright]? turned to sugar [Phillpotts]? sophisticated, like Chaucer's 'spiced conscience' [Jephson]? — Ar. and Pers. *qand*, sugar; *qandi*, made of sugar, sugared. *Skeat*. In *Timon of A.*, we have, IV, iii, 224, 'the cold brook candied with ice.' —

Can lay to bed forever; whiles you, doing thus,
To the perpetual wink for aye might put   280
This ancient morsel, this Sir Prudence, who
Should not upbraid our course. For all the rest,
They'll take suggestion as a cat laps milk;
They'll tell the clock to any business that
We say befits the hour.
    Sebastian.   Thy case, dear friend,
Shall be my precedent; as thou got'st Milan,
I'll come by Naples. Draw thy sword; one stroke
Shall free thee from the tribute which thou pay'st,
And I the king shall love thee.
    Antonio.   Draw together;
And when I rear my hand, do you the like,   290
To fall it on Gonzalo.
    Sebastian.   O! but—one word—
                              [*They talk apart.*

        Enter ARIEL, *with music and song.*

    Ariel. My master through his art foresees the danger
That you, his friend, are in, and sends me forth,—
For else his project dies,—to keep them living.
                        [*Sings in Gonzalo's ear.*

        While you here do snoring lie,
        Open-eyed conspiracy
          His time doth take.
        If of life you keep a care,
        Shake off slumber, and beware;
          Awake! Awake!   300

---

280. **perpetual** = continuous? continuing without break? Root PAT, to go; Gr. πατεῖν, patein, to tread; πάτος, patos, path; Lat. *per*, throughout.— **wink.** Line 211.— **aye.** Meaning? Pronunciation?— A. S. *ā*, Icel. *ei*, Gr. ἀεί, aei, ever, always; Lat. *ævum*, aye.— 282. **should.** Abbott, 322.— 283. **suggestion.** Shakes. apparently uses this word ten times in the sense of temptation. See our *Macbeth*, I, iii, 134.— 284. **tell.** A. S. *tellan*, to count. Line 15.— 287. **come by.** In *Acts*, xxvii, 16, and *Mer. of Ven.*, I, i, 3, 'come by' = get.— 290. **rear.** *Jul. Cæs.*, III, i, 30.— 291. **fall.** Abbott, 291.— 294. **them.** So the folio, referring probably to Alonso and Gonzalo. But many editors, as Dyce, Hudson, Clarke, etc., change *them* to 'thee.' Improvement? permissible change? "Ariel is half apostrophizing the sleeping Gonzalo and half talking to himself."

Antonio. Then let us both be sudden.
Gonzalo. [*Waking*] Now, good angels
Preserve the king! — [*To Sebastian and Antonio*] Why, how
 now? — [*To Alonso*] Ho, awake! —
[*To Sebastian and Antonio*] Why are you drawn? wherefore
 this ghastly looking?
Alonso. [*Waking*] What's the matter?
Sebastian. Whiles we stood here securing your repose,
Even now, we heard a hollow burst of bellowing
Like bulls, or rather lions; did 't not wake you?
It struck mine ear most terribly.
Alonso. I heard nothing.
Antonio. O, 'twas a din to fright a monster's ear,
To make an earthquake; sure, it was the roar 310
Of a whole herd of lions.
Alonso. Heard you this, Gonzalo?
Gonzalo. Upon mine honor, sir, I heard a humming, —
And that a strange one too, — which did awake me.
I shak'd you, sir, and cried; as mine eyes open'd,
I saw their weapons drawn: — there was a noise,
That's verily. 'Tis best we stand upon our guard,
Or that we quit this place; let's draw our weapons.
Alonso. Lead off this ground; and let's make further
 search
For my poor son.
Gonzalo. Heavens keep him from these beasts!
For he is, sure, i' the island.
Alonso. Lead away. 320
Ariel. Prospero my lord shall know what I have done;
So, king, go safely on to seek thy son. [*Exeunt.*

W. A. Wright. — 301-304. Staunton suggested, and Dyce, adding stage directions, adopted the reading which we give, and which Furness pronounces 'admirable.' — 303. **drawn.** *Abbott*, 374. Repeatedly in *Shakes.* applied to persons who *have drawn*. — 314. **shak'd.** Five times in *Shakes.* for *shook*. *Abbott*, 343. — 316. **that's verily.** So 'that's worthily,' *Coriol.*, IV, i, 53. Pope changed *verily* to 'verity.' *Abbott*, 78. — **best we stand.** So Milton's *Comus*, 487.

In this scene, why is prose used in banter or mockery, but metre in utterances of grief or sorrow? Do dignity and emotion find better expression in blank verse than in prose? Does humor? — Do Antonio and Gonzalo use mockery or scorn in order to rid themselves of uneasy feelings of inferiority? — Compare the plot to murder Alonso with that in *Macbeth* to murder Duncan. Note in each Shakespeare's 'manner of familiarizing a mind to the suggestion of guilt.'

Scene II. *Another Part of the Island.*

Enter Caliban, *with a burthen of wood. A noise of thunder heard.*

Caliban. All the infections that the sun sucks up
From bogs, fens, flats, on Prosper fall, and make him
By inch-meal a disease! His spirits hear me,
And yet I needs must curse. But they'll nor pinch,
Fright me with urchin-shows, pitch me i' the mire,
Nor lead me, like a firebrand, in the dark
Out of my way, unless he bid 'em: but
For every trifle they are set upon me;
Sometime like apes, that mow and chatter at me,
And after bite me; then like hedgehogs, which   10
Lie tumbling in my barefoot way, and mount
Their pricks at my footfall; sometime am I
All wound with adders, who with cloven tongues
Do hiss me into madness. —

Enter Trinculo.

Lo, now, lo!
Here comes a spirit of his, and to torment me
For bringing wood in slowly. I'll fall flat;
Perchance he will not mind me.   17

Trinculo. Here's neither bush nor shrub, to bear off any weather at all, and another storm brewing; I hear it sing i'

Scene II. 1. **sun sucks up.** Any trace here of a superstition or fancy among the ignorant that "the sun is drawing water," when his slant rays seem to stream through the clouds?—3. **inch-meal.** A. S. *mael*, piece, share, portion; dative case, *maelum*, in pieces, separately. So 'limb-meal,' *Cymbeline*, II, iv, 146. We use 'piecemeal.' "Twice I was shot all into inch pieces." *Serg't Reed.*—5. **urchin-shows.** Note, I, ii, 325; our ed. of *Comus*, line 845.—6. **firebrand** = *ignis fatuus?* See on 'played the Jack,' IV, i, 198.—9. **mow.** See stage direction, III, iii, 82; IV, i, 47.—Fr. *moue*, a pouting face; fr. O. Du. *mouwe*, the protruded under lip. *Brachet, Skeat.*—10. **after.** So III, ii, 144.—11. **mount.** 'The fire that mounts the liquor,' *Henry VIII*, I, i, 144; id. I, ii, 205.— Had Shakes. been reading Harsnet's *Declaration* (1603), "They (young girls supposed bewitched) make anticke faces, grin, mow, and mope like an ape, tumble like a hedge-hogge," etc.—13. **wound** = wounded? enwrapped (by adders 'wound' or twisted about me) [Johnson]?—**cloven.** *Macb.*, IV, i, 16; *Mid. N. Dr.*, II, iii, 9.—15. **and** = and comes? and that too [Abbott, 95, 96]?—19. **at all.** Does 'at all' modify *shrub? bear off?* or the wind. Yond same black cloud, yond huge one, looks like a foul bombard that would shed his liquor. If it should thunder as it did before, I know not where to hide my head; yond same cloud cannot choose but fall by pailfuls. — What have we here? a man or a fish? dead or alive? A fish: he smells like a fish; a very ancient and fishlike smell; a kind of, not of the newest, poor-john. A strange fish! Were I in England now, as once I was, and had but this fish painted, not a holiday fool there but would give a piece of silver: there would this monster make a man; any strange beast there makes a man. When they will not give a doit to relieve a lame beggar, they will lay out ten to see a dead Indian. Legged like a man! and his fins like arms! Warm, o' my troth! I do now let loose my opinion, hold it no longer; this is no fish, but an islander, that hath lately suffered by a thunderbolt. [*Thunder.*]

---

weather? — 20. **yond.** The Teutonic type is YENA, extended from Aryan base YA, that, *Skeat.* See on I, ii, 408. — 21. **foul** = unfair, vile? full? black with age and decayed — ready to fall to pieces [Rolfe]? Tyrwhitt surmised that 'foul' was by rustics pronounced like 'full.' Upton and Jervis would read 'full.' Furness suggests that "the force of 'foule,' as in the text, is not at once apparent." But is it not just like 'scurvy' before 'tune,' line 41? — *Lear,* III, ii, 24. — **bombard.** 'A cannon or great gun, and jocularly a large drinking vessel.' *Skeat.* 'A very large leathern drinking vessel.' *Halliwell.* So a soldier calls his whiskey flask a 'pocket pistol'! Hal terms Falstaff a 'huge bombard of sack,' *1 Henry IV,* II, iv, 16. — 26. **newest** = freshest? — **poor-john** = salt dry hake, a fish resembling the cod, but inferior; called *hake,* fr. Norweg. *hake,* hook, from its hook-shaped under-jaw. "I know not how it has happened that in the principal modern languages, John, or its equivalent, is a name of contempt, or at least of slight," says *Tyrwhitt.* Perhaps because the name was so common among the lower classes, and the average specimen of plebeian humanity was so poorly equipped? See John Bull, Johnny Crapaud, Mongolian Johnnie; *John-a-dreams, Hamlet,* II, ii, 55; IV, i, 197; Jack-o'-lantern, Jack Ketch, Jack-a-napes, jackstraw, jackass. — 26. **England.** Shakes. dearly loves to satirize good-naturedly his countrymen's foibles. *Othello,* II, iii, 65-68; *Mer. of Ven.,* I, ii, 58-66. — 29. **make a man.** Emphasis on *make?* Is the phrase still used? Foresaw Barnum? — 30. **doit.** Dutch *duit,* a copper coin, half farthing, eighth of a stiver? Perhaps Fr. *d'huit,* of eight, Lat. *octo,* eighth of a penny? Or Icel. *thveit,* a piece cut off (So Wb. *Int. Dict.*)? Or allied to *dot?* — Our *Mer. of Ven.,* I, iii, 130. — 31. **dead Indian.** Sir Martin Frobisher twice brought Indians to England, two of whom died there. The last time was in 1577, when he brought a man, a woman, and a child. "The captayne retayned two of these [Patagonian giants], which were youngest and best made." Eden's *Travels,* 1577. "They seem to have been sometimes exhibited embalmed, or even manufactured at home, as we see in line 61 [53], 'Do you put tricks upon 's with savages and men of Ind?'" *Phillpotts.* — See *Furness.* — 33. **let loose** = abandon? allow to be uttered? — **hold** = entertain? cling to? keep it back from being spoken? — 34. **suffered** = experienced

Alas, the storm is come again! my best way is to creep under his gaberdine; there is no other shelter hereabout. Misery acquaints a man with strange bedfellows. I will here shroud till the dregs of the storm be past.

Enter STEPHANO, *singing: a bottle in his hand.*

Stephano.   *I shall no more to sea, to sea,*
        Here shall I die ashore,—   40

This is a very scurvy tune to sing at a man's funeral. Well, here's my comfort.   [*Drinks.*

[Sings] *The master, the swabber, the boatswain, and I,*
        The gunner, and his mate,
   Lov'd Mall, Meg, and Marian, and Margery,
      But none of us car'd for Kate;
      For she had a tongue with a tang,
      Would cry to a sailor, Go hang!
   She loved not the savor of tar nor of pitch,
   Then, to sea, boys, and let her go hang!

This is a scurvy tune too; but here's my comfort. [*Drinks.*
  Caliban. Do not torment me!—O!   51
  Stephano. What's the matter? Have we devils here? Do you put tricks upon's with savages and men of Ind, ha? I have not scaped drowning to be afeard now of your four legs; for it hath been said, as proper a man as ever went on

---

suffering? suffered death [Wright, Deighton]? See 'suffered' in the Creeds in the *Book of Common Prayer.*—36. **gaberdine.** Span. *gabardina*, a coarse frock; *gaban*, a great coat. *Mer. of Ven.*, I, iii, 102.— 38. **shroud.** A. S. *scrud*, garment. Milton uses the word as a verb for find shelter or take shelter, in *Comus*, 316.—**dregs.** Refers to the liquor of the 'bombard' . . . the very last drop of the storm [Furness]? Is the newly arrived storm the dregs of the former?

41. **scurvy.** From the lack of anti-scorbutics, the word occurs to seamen more than to others?—43. **swabber** = deck-mopper or scrubber. Du. *zwabber*, the drudge of a ship; Swed. *svab*, a fire-brush; allied to *swap*, to strike, and to sweep. *Skeat.*—47. **tang** = sharp biting speech? high shrill tone [Meiklejohn]? twang, unpleasant tone [Wright]?—Imitative word, akin to *tinkle, tingle*, and perhaps to *twang*. *Skeat.*—48. **Yet a tailor might scratch her.** We should expect *sailor.*—where ere she did itch. So the folio.—53. **Ind.** So *Par. Lost*, ii, 2, and three times in *Shakes.* See on line 31.—**you** and **yours** in Stephano's drunken soliloquy are colloquial? addressed to some imaginary person? *Abbott*, 221.— 54. **scaped.** Fr. *échapper*, to escape. See our *Mer. of Ven.*, III, ii, 265. —55. **proper.** *Hebrews*, xi, 23; our *Mer. of Ven.*, I, ii, 62; *Jul. Cæs.*,

four legs cannot make him give ground; and it shall be said so again, while Stephano breathes at nostrils.

Caliban. The spirit torments me!—O! 58

Stephano. This is some monster of the isle with four legs, who had got, as I take it, an ague. Where the devil should he learn our language? I will give him some relief, if it be but for that. If I can recover him, and keep him tame, and get to Naples with him, he's a present for any emperor that ever trod on neat's-leather.

Caliban. Do not torment me, prithee; I'll bring my wood home faster.

Stephano. He's in his fit now, and does not talk after the wisest. He shall taste of my bottle; if he have never drunk wine afore, it will go near to remove his fit. If I can recover him and keep him tame, I will not take too much for him; he shall pay for him that hath him, and that soundly. 71

Caliban. Thou dost me yet but little hurt; thou wilt anon, I know it by thy trembling: now Prosper works upon thee.

Stephano. Come on your ways; open your mouth; here is that which will give language to you, cat. Open your mouth; this will shake your shaking, I can tell you, and that soundly: you cannot tell who's your friend; open your chaps again.

Trinculo. I should know that voice: it should be—but he is drowned; and these are devils!—O, defend me! 80

Stephano. Four legs and two voices! a most delicate monster! His forward voice, now, is to speak well of his friend; his backward voice is to utter foul speeches and to detract. If all the wine in my bottle will recover him, I will help

---

I, i, 25.—60. **the devil** = in the name of the devil, I ask? the devil help me?—64. **neat's** = bovine? See our *Jul. Cæs.*, I, i, 26; *Win. Tale*, I, ii, 124, 125.—69. **afore,** like 'afeard' in line 54, is repeatedly found in Shakes. Note the scientific knowledge implied in this "if he have never," etc.—**recover.** *Jul. Cæs.*, I, i, 24.—70. **too much,** etc. = no price will be too much [Malone]? I will not set a great price [too much] on him [spoken ironically]?—73. **trembling.** Sign of demoniac 'possession' or supernatural influence? See *Comedy of Errors*, IV, iv, 49, "Mark how he trembles in his ecstasy." In Harsnet's (1603) *Declaration*, "All the spirits with much ado being commanded to go down into her left foot, they did it with vehement trembling"; quoted by Furness.—75. **cat,** etc. "Alluding to the old proverb that 'good liquor will make a cat speak.'" Steevens. Any resemblance to a catfish implied?—76. **shake your shaking** = break up your ague?—77. **chaps** (from chops?) Skt. *kaf*, jaw; A.S. *ceaft*, the jowl. Akin to 'chew.'—81. **delicate.** He has his

his ague. Come.—Amen! I will pour some in thy other mouth.

Trinculo. Stephano.

Stephano. Doth thy other mouth call me? Mercy, mercy! This is a devil, and no monster: I will leave him; I have no long spoon.

Trinculo. Stephano! If thou beest Stephano, touch me, and speak to me; for I am Trinculo,—be not afeard,—thy good friend Trinculo. 92

Stephano. If thou beest Trinculo, come forth: I'll pull thee by the lesser legs; if any be Trinculo's legs, these are they. Thou art very Trinculo indeed! How camest thou to be the siege of this moon-calf? Can he vent Trinculos?

Trinculo. I took him to be killed with a thunder-stroke. —But art thou not drowned, Stephano? I hope, now, thou art not drowned. Is the storm overblown? I hid me under the dead moon-calf's gaberdine for fear of the storm. And art thou living, Stephano? O Stephano, two Neapolitans scaped? 102

Stephano. Prithee, do not turn me about; my stomach is not constant.

Caliban. These be fine things, an if they be not sprites. That's a brave god, and bears celestial liquor; I will kneel to him.

Stephano. How didst thou scape? How camest thou hither? swear, by this bottle, how thou camest hither. I escaped upon a butt of sack, which the sailors heaved o'erboard, by this bottle!—which I made of the bark of a tree with mine own hands, since I was cast ashore. 112

---

little grim joke.—85. **Amen** = stop drinking! [Steevens, Wright, Deighton]? Stephano is frightened and put to his religion, and 'Amen' is the best he can do towards praying [Hudson]? a benediction [Capell]?— 89. **long spoon.** "The Vice was made to associate with the Devil in the ancient Moralities [Morality plays], in which it was a piece of humor to make the Devil and Vice feed of the same custard or some such dish, the Devil on one side and the Vice on the other, with a spoon of vast length." Capell. "He must have a long spoon that eats with the devil," *Com. of Er.*, IV, iii, 58, 59.—95. **very Trinculo.** Lat. *verus*, true.—96. **siege** = seat; stool. So in *Meas. for M.*, IV, ii, 93. Lat. *sedes*, Fr. *siége*, a seat.— **moon-calf** = monstrosity, abortion, lifeless lump.—105. **an if.** *An* or *and* = if. "'And if' occurs on the same principle probably as 'most unkindest.'" *Furness.* Abbott, 103. For emphasis, like 'verily, verily'? —**sprites**, I, ii, 378.—109. **by this bottle.** Swear by what was most sacred?—110. **butt** = cask of 126 gals.?—**sack.** Gr. σάκκος, Lat. *saccus*, A.S. *sack*, a bag? a wine-skin? Better fr. Lat. *siccus*, Span. *seco*, Fr. *sec,*

Caliban. I'll swear, upon that bottle, to be thy true subject;
For the liquor is not earthly.

Stephano. Here; swear, then, how thou escapedst.

Trinculo. Swam ashore, man, like a duck; I can swim like a duck, I'll be sworn.

Stephano. Here, kiss the book. Though thou canst swim like a duck, thou art made like a goose.

Trinculo. O Stephano, hast any more of this? 120

Stephano. The whole butt, man; my cellar is in a rock by the sea-side, where my wine is hid. — How now, moon-calf! how does thine ague?

Caliban. Hast thou not dropped from heaven?

Stephano. Out o' the moon, I do assure thee; I was the man i' the moon when time was.

Caliban. I have seen thee in her, and I do adore thee;
My mistress show'd me thee, and thy dog, and thy bush.

Stephano. Come, swear to that; kiss the book: I will furnish it anon with new contents; swear. 130

Trinculo. By this good light, this is a very shallow monster! — I afeard of him! — A very weak monster! — The man i' the moon! — A most poor credulous monster! — Well drawn, monster, in good sooth!

Caliban. I'll show thee every fertile inch o' the island;
And I will kiss thy foot. I prithee, be my god.

Trinculo. By this light, a most perfidious and drunken monster! When's god's asleep, he'll rob his bottle.

Caliban. I'll kiss thy foot; I'll swear myself thy subject.

Stephano. Come on, then; down, and swear. 140

Trinculo. I shall laugh myself to death at this puppy-headed monster. A most scurvy monster! I could find in my heart to beat him —

---

dry; E. Eng. **seck**, a 'dry wine,' *vin sec?* sherry? Canary wine or white wines of Spain? See *Furness*.— 118. **the book** = the Bible? here the bottle?— 119. **goose.** Origin of the disparagement in bird names, as gull, loon, booby, etc.? Our *Macb.*, V, iii, 11. — 126. **man in the moon.** See II, i, 144. They fancied they saw in the moon the shape of a man, a lantern, and a bush; that the bush was the bundle of sticks (in *Numbers*, xv, 32, 33); the man, Cain; the dog, 'the foul fiend.' Some said that the bush represented the thorns and thistles that sprang up after 'the fall'! See in our *Mid. N. D.*, note on III, i, 52; also *M. N. D.*, V, i, 237.— 133. **well drawn** = a 'good pull' at the bottle?— 138. **rob** = steal [Allen, Schmidt, Deighton]? steal from [Wright]?— 141. **puppy-headed.** So we sometimes hear 'pig-headed,' 'bull-headed,' etc.— 143. **beat him** — The sentence is interrupted by Stephano's "Come, kiss," and

SCENE II.]   *THE TEMPEST.*   79

    Stephano. Come, kiss.
    Trinculo. But that the poor monster's in drink. An abominable monster!
    Caliban. I'll show thee the best springs; I'll pluck thee berries;
I'll fish for thee, and get thee wood enough.
A plague upon the tyrant that I serve!
I'll bear him no more sticks, but follow thee,   150
Thou wondrous man.
    Trinculo. A most ridiculous monster, to make a wonder of a poor drunkard!
    Caliban. I prithee, let me bring thee where crabs grow;
And I with my long nails will dig thee pig-nuts,
Show thee a jay's nest, and instruct thee how
To snare the nimble marmoset. I'll bring thee
To clustering filberts; and sometimes I'll get thee
Young scamels from the rock. Wilt thou go with me?
    Stephano. I prithee now, lead the way without any more talking. — Trinculo, the king and all our company else being drowned, we will inherit here. — Here, bear my bottle. — Fellow Trinculo, we'll fill him by and by again.   163

---

then is resumed by Trinculo's adding "but that the poor," etc. — 144. **kiss.** What? bottle? foot? — 154. **crabs?** Small sour apples? shellfish? — 155. **pig-nuts** = ground-nuts such as pigs root up? the round brown nut (*bunium flexuosum*) white inside and of a pleasant nutty flavor [*Grindon's Shakes. Flora*]? peanuts? — 157. **marmoset** = little American monkey? Lat. *minimus*, very small; O. Fr. *merme*, tiny; *marmot*, puppet, ape. *Worc. Brachet*, following *Littré*, derives it from *marmoretum*, a little marble figure, fr. *marmor*, marble. The *Rue des Marmousets* in Paris was in Mediæv. Latin *Vicus Marmoretorum.* — Sir John Mandeville and other English writers mention the animal. — 159. **scamels.** This word has been a standing puzzle. Among the proposed emendations are *shamois* (or *chamois*), *sea-malls, sea-mells, sea-gulls, sea-mews, stannels, scams, samols, samphire, squirrels, seegells, staniels, scalions, sarcels, stamels, scambles, limpets, muscles, conies, chamals, sea-owls*.' "The female Bar-tailed Godwit is called a 'scamel' by the gunners of Blakeney. But . . . this bird is not a rock-breeder." Stevenson's *Birds of Norfolk*, quoted by Wright. — The average scholar, in the midst of these perplexities, may well adopt the modest attitude of Furness, who says: "For my part I unblushingly confess that I do not know what 'scamels' are, and that I prefer to retain the word in the text and to remain in utter, invincible ignorance. From the very beginning of the play we know that the scene lies in an enchanted island. Is this to be forgotten? Since the air is full of sweet sounds, why may not the rocks be inhabited by unknown birds of gay plumage or by vague animals of a grateful and appetising plumpness? Let the picture remain, of the dashing rocks, the stealthy, freckled whelp, and in the clutch of his long nails, a young and tender scamel." *Preface* to *Variorum Ed.* of *The Tempest*, p. viii. — 162. **inherit** = take possession? occupy? Often used for 'pos-

Caliban. [*Sings drunkenly*] Farewell, master; farewell, farewell!

Trinculo. A howling monster; a drunken monster!

Caliban. *No more dams I'll make for fish;*
Nor fetch in firing
At requiring;
Nor scrape trenchering, nor wash dish.
'Ban, 'Ban, Ca-caliban 170
Has a new master: — *get a new man.*

Freedom, high-day! high-day, freedom! freedom, high-day, freedom!

Stephano. O brave monster! Lead the way. [*Exeunt.*

---

sess' in *S.*, IV, i, 154. — 167. **trenchering.** Pope and nearly all subsequent editors have changed this to 'trencher,' to improve the poetry. But Caliban, drunk, was not an artist in verse! White objects to the curtailment on the ground, also, that "there is a drunken swing in the original line which is entirely lost in the precise curtailed rhythm."—172. **high-day!** So the folios. All the editors needlessly change this to *hey-day*, which is probably a corrupted form. 'High day' is found in *Mer. of Ven.*, II, ix, 97; also in *John*, xix, 31, "That sabbath day was an high day." It makes as good sense as *hey-day?* Why change it?—'Hey-day' is in *Hamlet*, II, iv, 69. In *Merry Wives*, III, ii, 58, 59, we read, "he speaks holiday." —171. **get** = become, or will become [Furness]? get thou (to Prospero) [Capell, Steevens]?

"Notice how a few bold strokes in this scene suffice to sketch the vices of a low civilization .. What a strange harmony there is between Caliban and the nature which surrounds him, and of which he is in some sense a part; whence a kind of grace, which places him as much above the drunken and graceless European as he is below Prospero and Miranda! Remark in Act III, iii, 130, how much more sensitive he is than they to sweetness of sound!" *Phillpotts.*

Caliban is in some respects a noble being; the poet has raised him far above contempt; he is a man in the sense of the imagination; all the images he uses are drawn from Nature and are highly poetical; they fit in with the images of Ariel. Caliban gives us images from the earth, Ariel from the air. Caliban talks of the difficulty of finding fresh water, of the situation of morasses, and of other circumstances which even brute instinct, without reason, could comprehend. No mean figure is employed, no mean passion displayed, beyond animal passion and repugnance to command. Coleridge's *Seven Lectures*, 1818.

ACT III.

Scene I. *Before Prospero's Cell.*

Enter Ferdinand, *bearing a log.*

Ferdinand. There be some sports are painful, and their labor
Delight in them sets off; some kinds of baseness
Are nobly undergone, and most poor matters
Point to rich ends. This my mean task
Would be as heavy to me as odious, but
The mistress which I serve quickens what's dead,
And makes my labors pleasures. O, she is
Ten times more gentle than her father's crabbed,
And he's compos'd of harshness! I must remove
Some thousands of these logs, and pile them up,   10
Upon a sore injunction. My sweet mistress
Weeps when she sees me work, and says such baseness
Had never like executor. I forget;
But these sweet thoughts do even refresh my labors,
Most busy, least, when I do it.

ACT III. Scene I. 1. **there be.** Use of 'be' determined by euphony [Furness]? *Abbott*, 300.—**painful** = causing pain? full of pains, i.e. painstaking? requiring the player to take pains or employ labor. [Phila. *Sh. Soc.*]?—" Oh, the holiness of their living and the painfulness of their preaching!" Fuller's *Holy State*, ii, 6.—2. **sets.** The folio has *set*. Rowe made the change which all subsequent editors have adopted. **sets off** = compensates? offsets? Subject nom. of *sets?* Malone quotes "The labor we delight in physics pain," *Macb.*, II, iii, 31.—**baseness** = vileness? humbleness?—3. **most poor** = poorest? a majority of poor?— 4. **point** = have a view? tend? are directed?—6. **which.** Interchangeable with *who? Abbott*, 265.—9. **compos'd.** Emphatic here?— 13. Scan. Should 'never' be shortened to 'ne'er'? 'executor' acc. on 3d syl.?—**forget.** What?—15. **most busy, least, when I do it.** The 1st folio has *lest;* the others, *least.* "Compositors, we know, were apt to spell phonetically, accordingly we find them spelling *least, lest,* which is a pretty good guide to the pronunciation of the word." *Furness*, in footnote in his *Var. Ed.* of *Mid. N. Dr.*, p. 225.—" This passage has received a greater number of emendations, and staggers under a heavier weight of comment than, I believe, any other in Shakespeare." *Furness.*

Enter MIRANDA, *and* PROSPERO *at a distance.*

Miranda.   Alas! now, pray you,
Work not so hard; I would the lightning had
Burnt up those logs that you are enjoin'd to pile!
Pray, set it down, and rest you; when this burns,
'Twill weep for having wearied you. My father
Is hard at study; pray, now, rest yourself;   20
He's safe for these three hours.
   Ferdinand.   O most dear mistress,
The sun will set before I shall discharge
What I must strive to do.
   Miranda.   If you'll sit down,
I'll bear your logs the while. Pray, give me that;
I'll carry it to the pile.
   Ferdinand.   No, precious creature;
I had rather crack my sinews, break my back,
Than you should such dishonor undergo,
While I sit lazy by.

See the twelve solid pages, 144–156, in his *Var. Ed.* In the magazine *Shakespeariana*, N.Y., March, 1884, the present editor suggested what he believes to be the true interpretation. It is in the main quoted by Furness, page 154, *Var. Ed.* "Punctuate thus: Most busy, least, when I do it. Interpret thus: Most busy least busy (i.e. least conscious of being busy) when I do this work." In other words, when I think of Miranda and her love, toil is even *restful*. I forget the toil for the time, but her love turns the toil to refreshment, to pleasure. No change in the text is necessary. The line is the exact converse of Macbeth's "The rest is labor that is not used for you," *Macb.*, I, iv, 44. With Macbeth repose is labor; with Ferdinand, labor is repose!—'When I do it' *may* mean, 'When I forget'; i.e. 'When I am oblivious of all but Miranda.' We may add that A.S. *bysgian* often means to *fatigue*. See note on line 16.—Furness, after wading through the tremendous pages of comment, which he has skilfully condensed into twelve, gives his own interpretation as follows: "Ferdinand has been neglecting his task to think of Miranda; then, recollecting himself, says, in effect, I am forgetting my work—but when I do *thus forget*, my mind so teems with thoughts that I am really most busy when I seem to be least busy, and by these sweet thoughts I am even refreshed for my work."—Note the paradoxes: in this connection, Phillpotts cites *Sonnet* xxvii.—16. **Work not so hard.** We may perhaps suppose that, just before, absorbed in thinking of Miranda, he had forgotten his task and stood motionless for a minute; but now had begun it again with renewed heroic energy under the inspiration and joy of reciprocated love. At this instant she approaches unseen, and, beholding his intense toil, she exclaims "Alas, now, pray you, work not so hard," etc.—19. **weep.** When green or wet wood burns, drops like hot tears are often forced out at the end of the log! Would Francis Bacon have so personified?—21. **safe.** Like *Hamlet's* 'safely stowed'!

Miranda. It would become me
As well as it does you; and I should do it
With much more ease, for my good will is to it, 30
And yours it is against.
   Prospero. Poor worm, thou art infected!
This visitation shows it.
   Miranda. You look wearily.
   Ferdinand. No, noble mistress; 'tis fresh morning with
   me
When you are by at night. I do beseech you, —
Chiefly that I might set it in my prayers, —
What is your name?
   Miranda. Miranda. — O my father,
I have broken your hest to say so!
   Ferdinand. Admir'd Miranda!
Indeed the top of admiration, worth
What's dearest to the world! Full many a lady
I have eyed with best regard, and many a time 40
The harmony of their tongues hath into bondage
Brought my too diligent ear. For several virtues
Have I lik'd several women, never any
With so full soul but some defect in her
Did quarrel with the noblest grace she owed,
And put it to the foil; but you, O you,

Hamlet, IV, ii, 1. — 31. **against.** *Abbott*, 203. — 32. **wearily.** The use of an adverb for an adjective with 'look' is not uncommon in *Shakes.* See 'look merrily' in *Jul. Cæs.*, II, i, 224; *Two Gen. of V.*, II, i, 25; *Much Ado*, II, i, 75. — 33. **fresh morning.** *Mer. of V.*, V, i, 127, 128; Sonnet xliii. — 35. **set.** Metaphor from the jeweler's art? *Cymb.*, I, iii, 34, 35. — 37. **hest.** I, ii, 274. — 38. **top of admiration.** Ferdinand seems to understand Latin; for *Miranda* = must be admired, or must be wondered at. — 42. **diligent** = loving? attentive? assiduous? Lat. *di-* or *dis-*, apart, *legĕre*, to choose; *diligĕre*, to choose between, select; love. *Skeat.* — **several** = a few of? a number of? separate? individual? — Lat. *se-*, apart; *parāre*, to provide; *separāre*, to separate. V, i, 232; *Comus*, 25; *Nativity Ode*, 234. — 45. **owed.** I, ii, 405. *Own* (ow-en) is orig. 'possessed.' — 46. **put it to the foil.** = compel it to stand on the defensive (metaphor from fencing) [Hudson]? foiled or disparaged ('foil' being from 'fouler,' to trample under foot) [Meiklejohn]? as we say, put her to the blush, cause her to blush [Deighton]? — Says Phillpotts, "There is difficulty in making out clearly the various senses of the word 'foil.' When Hamlet says, 'I'll be your foil, Laertes,' he means, 'I will be like the worthless *leaf* which sets off a jewel.' This first is fr. Fr. *feuille*, Lat. *folium*, a leaf. The foil with which Hamlet fights is, of course, a blunted weapon, and with it he hopes to 'foil' Laertes. We can, perhaps, account for both these latter senses from the O. Fr. '*De tes commandemenz ne foliai* (I did not go astray from thy commandments)'; whence also *affoler* is said of

So perfect and so peerless, are created
Of every creature's best!
    Miranda.   I do not know
One of my sex, no woman's face remember,
Save, from my glass, mine own; nor have I seen   50
More that I may call men than you, good friend,
And my dear father. How features are abroad,
I am skilless of; but, by my modesty,
The jewel in my dower, I would not wish
Any companion in the world but you!
Nor can imagination form a shape,
Besides yourself, to like of! — But I prattle
Something too wildly, and my father's precepts
I therein do forget.
    Ferdinand.   I am, in my condition,
A prince, Miranda; I do think, a king; —   60
I would, not so! — and would no more endure
This wooden slavery than to suffer
The flesh-fly blow my mouth. Hear my soul speak:
The very instant that I saw you, did

---

a compass needle which will *not point true;* so that a 'foil' is not an unnatural name for that which has had its point blunted, and therefore cannot accurately point at anything. 'To foil a lance thrust' is, in the same way, *to turn it aside, to make it go astray;* and the word when generalized comes to mean to 'defeat the attacks of an adversary.'" — 47, 48. **created of every creature's best.** A favorite thought with Shakespeare. *As Y. L. I.,* III, ii, 157-160; *Winter's Tale,* V, i, 14, 15. The reader will be reminded of the composite masterpiece of Apelles or that of Zeuxis, or the make-up of Pandora. Steevens refers to Sidney's *Arcadia,* where the beasts, by Jupiter's permission, made themselves a king so compounded!

53. **skilless.** Milton (*Areopagitica,* our *Masterpieces,* pp. 229, 242) twice uses skill as a verb. Icel. *skilja,* to divide, distinguish; *skil,* distinction, discernment. *Twelfth N.,* III, iii, 9. — 57. **besides** = abstractedly from, over and above [Schmidt]? other than? in comparison with? — **like of** — like? — *Abbott,* 177; *Much Ado,* V, iv, 59. — 58. **something** = some matter? somewhat? in some degree? I, ii, 413; *Abbott,* 68. — 62. **wooden** = pertaining to these logs? dull, stupid? 'Wood' suggests poor material? So we say 'blockhead'! — **to suffer.** Supply 'endure'? *Abbott,* 350. — 62. As to the metre of this line, Abbott, 478, and other precisians declare that the *er* final seems to have been sometimes pronounced with a kind of 'burr,' which produced the effect of an additional syllable! Abbott accordingly marks the line thus:

         This woód | en slá | very, thán | to súff | ér.

This wooden slavery to supposed metrical law is dreadful, and, out of Ireland, where the *r* has everything its own way, incredible. Better make a long pause after 'slavery'? — 63. **blow** = defile, pollute [Deighton]? lay

My heart fly to your service; there resides,
To make me slave to it; and for your sake
Am I this patient logman.
　　Miranda.　　　　　　　　Do you love me?
　　Ferdinand. O heaven! O earth! bear witness to this sound,
And crown what I profess with kind event,
If I speak true; if hollowly, invert
What best is boded me to mischief! I,
Beyond all limit of what else i' the world,
Do love, prize, honor you.
　　Miranda.　　　　　　　　I am a fool
To weep at what I am glad of.
　　Prospero.　　　　　　　　Fair encounter
Of two most rare affections! Heavens rain grace
On that which breeds between 'em!
　　Ferdinand.　　　　　　　　Wherefore weep you?
　　Miranda. At mine unworthiness, that dare not offer
What I desire to give, and much less take
What I shall die to want. But this is trifling;
And all the more it seeks to hide itself,
The bigger bulk it shows. Hence, bashful cunning!
And prompt me, plain and holy innocence!
I am your wife, if you will marry me;
If not, I'll die your maid: to be your fellow
You may deny me, but I'll be your servant,
Whether you will or no.

---

maggot eggs upon [Hudson]? — *Wint. T.*, IV, iii, 771. — 69. **event.** Lat. *e*, out; *venire, ventum*, to come. — 70. **hollowly.** *Meas. for M.*, II, iii, 23. How came 'hollow' to mean insincere? — 71. **boded.** A. S. *bod*, message; *bodian*, to announce. Is the sense now uniformly unfavorable? — 72. **what** = whatsoever [Hudson]? anything [Wright]? — 73, 74. **fool,** etc. Steevens, speaking of Shakespeare's preëminent naturalness, says, "It was necessary in support of the character of Miranda to make her appear unconscious that excess of sorrow and excess of joy find alike their relief in tears." *Macb.*, I, iv, 33-35. — 75. **affections** = attachments? — Phillpotts interprets thus: "What a meeting between such tears and such joy! May the heavens rain grace upon the love which grows between them!" — *Lear*, IV, iii, 16-21. — 78. **what.** Betrothal? marriage? — Capell says *it* and *itself* in line 80 relate to what Miranda's "delicacy does not admit of naming, — love." — 84. **your maid** = a maid for your sake; i.e. living unmarried all my life [Deighton]? maid-servant [Rolfe, Meiklejohn]? 'Maid' in the sense of female servant is not uncommon in New England villages. — **fellow.** I, ii, 415. "Good hay, sweet hay hath no fellow," says Bottom when 'translated' to an ass. *Mid. N. Dr.*, IV, i, 31. — 'Fellow' was used of both sexes. Our *Jul. Cæs.*, III, i, 62. — 85. **servant.** A

Ferdinand.   My mistress, dearest,
And I thus humble ever.
  Miranda.   My husband, then?
  Ferdinand. Ay, with a heart as willing
As bondage e'er of freedom; here's my hand.
  Miranda. And mine, with my heart in't: and now fare-
    well
Till half an hour hence.
  Ferdinand.   A thousand thousand!   91
       [*Exeunt Ferdinand and Miranda.*
  Prospero. So glad of this as they I cannot be,
Who are expris'd with all; but my rejoicing
At nothing can be more. I'll to my book,
For yet ere supper-time must I perform
Much business appertaining.   [*Exit.*

Scene II. *Another Part of the Island.*

Enter Caliban, Stephano, *and* Trinculo.

  Stephano. Tell not me:—when the butt is out, we will drink water; not a drop before: therefore bear up, and board 'em.—Servant-monster, drink to me.

---

strikingly similar passage is quoted by Phillpotts from *Catullus*, lxiv, 158–163. Douce and Singer think Shakes. had in mind the old poem of 'The Nut-brown Maid.'—87. **thus humble.** Kneeling?—88. **willing** = wishing? desirous?—91. **thousand thousand.** Shakes. is fond of the literal sense. *To fare* is to go; *farewell* = 'speed well,' prosper?—93. **are.** Hudson dares to change this to *am!* Many editors follow Theobald in printing 'withal' instead of *with all.*—94. **book.** Much importance attaches to *books* in this play. See in the next scene, lines 84–90; also, I, ii, 109, 166–168; V, i, 57.

"The whole courting scene," says Coleridge, "in the beginning of the third act, is a masterpiece; and the first dawn of disobedience in the mind of Miranda to the command of her father is very finely drawn, so as to seem the working of the Scriptural command, *Thou shalt leave father and mother*, etc. Oh, with what exquisite purity this scene is conceived and executed! Shakespeare may sometimes be gross, but I boldly say that he is always moral and modest. Alas! in this, our day, decency of manners is preserved at the expense of morality of heart, and delicacies for vice are allowed whilst grossness against it is hypocritically, or at least morbidly, condemned."

Scene II. 1. **Tell not me.** Trinculo carried the bottle? II, ii, 162. Had he been talking temperance?—2. **bear up** take your course, sail up [Rolfe, Schmidt]? put the helm up and keep the vessel off her course [Wright, Hudson, following Admiral Smyth's Sailor's Word-Book]? make for them [Meiklejohn]?—3. **board 'em** = enter their ship by force. Whose ship?—**servant-monster.** Ben Jonson in his induction to *Bar-*

Trinculo. Servant-monster! the folly of this island! They say there's but five upon this isle: we are three of them; if th'other two be brained like us, the State totters.
Stephano. Drink, servant-monster, when I bid thee; thy eyes are almost set in thy head.
Trinculo. Where should they be set else? he were a brave monster indeed, if they were set in his tail. 10
Stephano. My man-monster hath drowned his tongue in sack: for my part, the sea cannot drown me; I swam, ere I could recover the shore, five and thirty leagues off and on, by this light!— Thou shalt be my lieutenant, monster, or my standard.
Trinculo. Your lieutenant, if you list; he's no standard.
Stephano. We'll not run, Monsieur Monster.
Trinculo. Nor go neither; but you'll lie, like dogs, and yet say nothing neither.
Stephano. Moon-calf, speak once in thy life, if thou beest a good moon-calf. 21
Caliban. How does thy honor? Let me lick thy shoe. I'll not serve him, he is not valiant.
Trinculo. Thou liest, most ignorant monster; I am in case to justle a constable. Why, thou debosh'd fish, thou, was there ever a man a coward that hath drunk so much sack as I to-day? Wilt thou tell a monstrous lie, being but half a fish and half a monster?
Caliban. Lo, how he mocks me! wilt thou let him, my lord?
Trinculo. Lord, quoth he!— That a monster should be such a natural! 30

---

tholomew Fair, written between 1612 and 1614, appears to ridicule this term. Thus helps fix the date of this play?— 4: **the folly,** etc. Does he mean that Caliban is a fool? or that Stephano has become one? or that all three are idiots?— 6. **brained** = deprived, by violence, of brains? possessed of brains?— Line 85.— 8. **set** = fixed (in a vacant stare as if 'dead drunk')? See *1 Kings*, xiv, 4; *Twelfth N.*, V, i, 190, 191.— 13. **off and on** = at intervals? more or less? back and forth?— 14. **standard.** So 'ensign' is sometimes used for 'ensign-bearer,' 'trumpet,' for 'trumpeter'; Fr. 'guidon,' cavalry flag, for him who carries it.— Note the verbal play on *standard*, Caliban being unable to stand?— 15. **you list** = it please you? *You* is said to be in the dative case.— 17. **go** = walk? proceed?— **case** = situation? condition?— 25. **debosh'd.** Fr. *débaucher*, to take away the balks (i.e. beams) of a building. *Brachet.* *Worc.* gives *de*, negative, and Fr. *bauche*, a rank, course of stones, balk or beam, the idea being 'that of removing the supports of a house.' The spelling in the text shows the pronunciation in Shakespeare's time?— 26, 27, 30, 31. **monstrous . . . natural.** Note the quibbles.— **natural.** Has this word

Caliban. Lo, lo, again! bite him to death, I prithee.

Stephano. Trinculo, keep a good tongue in your head; if you prove a mutineer, — the next tree! The poor monster's my subject, and he shall not suffer indignity.

Caliban. I thank my noble lord. Wilt thou be pleas'd To hearken once again to the suit I made to thee?

Stephano. Marry, will I: kneel and repeat it; I will stand, and so shall Trinculo.

Enter ARIEL, *invisible.*

Caliban. As I told thee before, I am subject to a tyrant, A sorcerer, that by his cunning hath cheated me 40 Of the island.

Ariel. Thou liest.

Caliban. Thou liest, thou jesting monkey, thou; I would my valiant master would destroy thee! I do not lie.

Stephano. Trinculo, if you trouble him any more in's tale, by this hand, I will supplant some of your teeth.

Trinculo. Why, I said nothing.

Stephano. Mum, then, and no more. — Proceed.

Caliban. I say, by sorcery he got this isle; From me he got it. If thy greatness will, 50 Revenge it on him, for I know thou dar'st, But this thing dare not.

Stephano. That's most certain.

Caliban. Thou shalt be lord of it, and I'll serve thee.

Stephano. How now shall this be compass'd? Canst thou bring me to the party?

---

still the sense 'fool'? How did it ever get such a meaning? — 32. **again** = gibing at me [Deighton]? — **bite.** Very significant word! — 37. **marry** = By Mary? Mary help me? — Sound of *a* in *Maria?*
42. Stephano and Caliban think "Thou liest" to be spoken by Trinculo? — 48. **jesting monkey.** Wears Trinculo the garb of the professional jester or court fool? — 46. **by this hand.** An oath? a means, instrument or mode of 'supplanting'? Line 67. In *Twelfth N.*, I, iii, 31, we read, "By this hand, they are scoundrels." Any appropriateness in swearing by the hand? — Lat. *sub*, under; *planta*, sole of the foot; *supplantare*, to put something under the sole of the foot, to trip up the heels, to overthrow. *Skeat.* — 50. **mum.** Imitative? For the subjective internal force of the sound, see our *Masterpieces in Eng. Lit.*, pp. 40, 61. — 55. **compassed.** Stephano feels and talks 'big'? So he says 'party'! —

Caliban. Yea, yea, my lord; I'll yield him thee asleep, Where thou mayst knock a nail into his head.

Ariel. Thou liest; thou canst not.

Caliban. What a pied ninny's this! Thou scurvy patch!—
I do beseech thy greatness, give him blows, 61
And take his bottle from him: when that's gone,
He shall drink nought but brine; for I'll not show him
Where the quick freshes are.

Stephano. Trinculo, run into no further danger; interrupt the monster one word further, and, by this hand, I'll turn my mercy out o' doors, and make a stock-fish of thee.

Trinculo. Why, what did I? I did nothing. I'll go farther off.

Stephano. Didst thou not say he lied? 70

Ariel. Thou liest.

Stephano. Do I so? take thou that. [*Beats him.*] As you like this, give me the lie another time.

Trinculo. I did not give the lie. Out o' your wits, and hearing too?—A pox o' your bottle! this can sack and drinking do.—A murrain on your monster, and the devil take your fingers!

Caliban. Ha, ha, ha!

Stephano. Now, forward with your tale.—Prithee, stand farther off. 80

Caliban. Beat him enough; after a little time I'll beat him too.

Stephano. Stand farther.—Come, proceed.

---

58. **knock a nail.** *Judges*, iv, 21, 22. Has Miranda taught Caliban Bible stories? I, ii, 352; II, ii, 128.—60. **pied.** Lat. *pica*, a magpie; fr. root *pi*, imitative, a *pica* being a chirper. Any allusion to the magpie's colors?—**ninny**, fr. Gaelic *neoni*, a fool, or shortened from *nincompoop* (i.e. *non compos mentis*, not sound of mind)? or fr. Ital. *ninno*, a child; *ninna*, a lullaby to rock infants to sleep. *Worc.*, *Skeat*, etc.—**patch.** Named from his dress? See our *Mer. of Ven.*, II, iv, 45.—64. **quick freshes.** In I, ii, 462, we have 'fresh-brook muscles.' Nowhere but here is 'fresh' used for sweet-water springs. **Quick** as in *Hamlet*, V, i, 120; *2 Tim.*, iv, 1, etc.—67. **stock-fish.** In *1 Henry IV*, II, iv, 228, Falstaff addresses Hal, "You starveling, you eel-skin, you dried neat's tongue, you stock-fish!" In Ben Jonson's *Every Man in His Humor*, 1598, we find "Thou wilt be beaten like a stock-fish." The word is said to mean dried cod, which was beaten before boiling. "*Je te frotteray à double carrillon*, I will beat thee like a stock-fish." Hollyband's *French Dict.*, 1593.—72. **as** = according as? if?—76. **murrain.** Lat. *mori*, to die. *Exodus*, ix, 3.

Caliban. Why, as I told thee, 'tis a custom with him
I' the afternoon to sleep; there thou mayst brain him,
Having first seiz'd his books, or with a log
Batter his skull, or paunch him with a stake,
Or cut his weasand with thy knife. Remember
First to possess his books, for without them
He's but a sot, as I am, nor hath not
One spirit to command; they all do hate him
As rootedly as I. Burn but his books.
He has brave utensils, — for so he calls them, —
Which, when he has a house, he'll deck withal.
And that most deeply to consider is
The beauty of his daughter. He himself
Calls her a nonpareil; I never saw a woman,
But only Sycorax my dam and she;
But she as far surpasseth Sycorax
As great'st does least.
   Stephano. Is it so brave a lass?
   Caliban. Ay, lord.
   Stephano. Monster, I will kill this man; his daughter
and I will be king and queen, — save our graces! — and
Trinculo and thyself shall be viceroys. Dost thou like the
plot, Trinculo?
   Trinculo. Excellent.
   Stephano. Give me thy hand: I am sorry I beat thee;
but, while thou livest, keep a good tongue in thy head.
   Caliban. Within this half hour will he be asleep;
Wilt thou destroy him then?
   Stephano. Ay, on mine honor.

---

84. **there.** In his cell? in his sleep? — **brain.** Line 6. — 85. **books.** I, ii, 165-168. — 86. **paunch.** Like *brain*, 84? — 87. **weasand.** Perhaps an initial *h* has been lost, so that *weasand*, the form being evidently that of a pres. participle, is lit. 'the wheezing thing,' the windpipe. *Skeat, Worc.* — 89. **sot.** A. S. *sot*, foolish; Fr. *sot*, fool; Sp. *zote*, blockhead. Cotgrave's *Fr. and Eng. Dict.*, 1660, defines *sot* as '*asse, dunce*, dullard, blockhead . . . also a foole.' — 91. **but** = only, in two senses [Wright]? — 92. **utensils.** Milton, *Par. Reg.*, iii, 336, appears to accent this word on 1st syl. — 94. **that . . . consider** = that which is . . . to be considered? *Abbott*, 244, 359, 405. — 96. **non-pareil.** See our *Macb.*, III. iv, 19. — 97. **Sycorax.** I, ii, 258. — **she.** Shakes., it is said, nine times omits the inflection of 'she.' *Abbott*, 211. Furness's *Othello*, IV, ii, 5. "Mere carelessness on Shakespeare's part." *R. G. White.* — 99. **brave.** I, ii, 6. — 100. **Ay, lord.** As usual, the folio has *I.* — **She will become thy bed, I warrant.** *Become* = adorn. — 101. **And bring thee forth brave brood.** Brave as in 99, and I, ii, 6.

Ariel. This will I tell my master.
Caliban. Thou mak'st me merry; I am full of pleasure. Let us be jocund; will you troll the catch
You taught me but while-ere?
Stephano. At thy request, monster, I will do reason, any reason. — Come on, Trinculo, let us sing. [*Sings.*

*Flout 'em and scout 'em, and scout 'em and flout 'em;
Thought is free.*

Caliban. That's not the tune.
[*Ariel plays the tune on a tabor and pipe.*
Stephano. What is this same? 120
Trinculo. This is the tune of our catch, played by the picture of Nobody.
Stephano. If thou beest a man, show thyself in thy likeness; if thou beest a devil, take't as thou list.
Trinculo. O, forgive me my sins!
Stephano. He that dies pays all debts; I defy thee. — Mercy upon us!
Caliban. Art thou afeard?
Stephano. No, monster, not I.
Caliban. Be not afeared; the isle is full of noises, 130
Sounds and sweet airs, that give delight and hurt not.

---

113. **troll** = round out glibly or volubly [Hudson]? sing in rollicking fashion [Meiklejohn]? run glibly over (an imitative word) [Wright]? sing irregularly [Skeat]? — French *trôler*, to lead, drag; O. Fr. *troller*, Ger. *trollen*, Welsh *trolio*, Mid. E. *trollen*, to roll. "To troll the bowl is to send it round, to circulate it." *Skeat*. — **catch.** 'A part-song or round, in which one singer catches up the words and air after another.' "The words of one part are made to answer, or *catch* the other; as 'Ah! how, Sophia,' sung like 'a house o' fire,' 'Burney's History,' like 'burn his history,' etc." Chappell's *Popular Music of the Olden Time.* — 114. **while-ere** = erewhile, some time ago? — A. S. *aer*, before; *hwil*, time. — *Abbott*, 137. — 118. **Thought is free.** Note what Dowden (*Shakespeare — His Mind and Art*, 373, 376) says of Shakespeare's treatment, in this play, of the question, 'What is freedom?' — 119. **not the tune.** Caliban's ear better than Stephano's? — **tabor** = a sort of drum (beaten with one stick)? a hoop with sheepskin stretched tight over it, making a kind of drum like a tambourine? — 121. **picture of Nobody.** Knight reproduces the old picture of 'No Body,' a figure of a head, arms, legs, without a trunk (body). It often appeared on sign-boards. In 1606 such a picture was prefixed to a comedy (privately reprinted in 1877) entitled '*No-body and Some-body*.' Some of Cruikshank's caricatures are based on this idea. — 124. **take't as thou list** = take what shape pleases thee [Rolfe]? take my remark as you may please [Deighton]? — 130-139. This savage has much poetry in his soul. — 134. **that**, etc. '*That*,' without *so* before it, often

Sometimes a thousand twangling instruments
Will hum about mine ears; and sometimes voices,
That, if I then had wak'd after long sleep,
Will make me sleep again: and then, in dreaming,
The clouds methought would open, and show riches
Ready to drop upon me; that, when I wak'd,
I cried to dream again.

Stephano. This will prove a brave kingdom to me, where
I shall have my music for nothing. 140

Caliban. When Prospero is destroy'd.

Stephano. That shall be by and by; I remember the story.

Trinculo. The sound is going away; let's follow it, and after do our work.

Stephano. Lead, monster; we'll follow. — I would I could see this taborer; he lays it on.

Trinculo. Wilt come? [*To Caliban.*] I'll follow Stephano.
[*Exeunt.*

SCENE III. *Another Part of the Island.*

Enter ALONSO, SEBASTIAN, ANTONIO, GONZALO, ADRIAN, FRANCISCO, *and others.*

Gonzalo. By'r lakin! I can go no further, sir;
My old bones ache: here's a maze trod, indeed,
Through forth-rights and meanders! By your patience,
I needs must rest me.

---

expresses *result.* I, ii, 85. — 142. **by and by** = immediately; presently? *Matt.,* xiii, 21; *Luke,* xxi, 9; often in *Shakes.,* as *Hamlet,* III, ii, 360, 362. — 147. **Stephano.** The folio puts 'Stephano' in italics with no pause before it. Steevens (1778) inserted a comma, as if Stephano were addressed. Trinculo and Stephano incline to follow the music, Stephano going foremost. Caliban, a little disgusted, tarries. Trinculo turns to him and says, "Wilt come? I'll follow Stephano."
SCENE III. 1. **By'r lakin!** — *Ladykin* = little lady; i.e. the Virgin Mary. Minced oaths and dimin. nouns were common. So *zounds* (for 'God's wounds'), *sblood* (for 'God's blood'); *sdeath,* etc. The *-kin* is affectionate, as we express by the phrase '*precious* little.' — 2. **ache.** I, ii, 368. The 1st folio has 'akes,' which Abbott, 333, thinks to be the old North-of-England 3d pers. plural. — **maze** = artificially constructed labyrinth [Halliwell]? — Mid. E. *masen,* to confuse, puzzle. Prob. the orig. sense was 'to be lost in thought,' to dream, from the root MA, to think (shorter form of MAN), akin to *mind.* Man is the *thinking* animal. *Skeat.* — 3. **forth-rights** = paths at right angles [Phillpotts]? straight paths [Knight, Wright, Hudson, Rolfe, etc.]? straight lines [Hunter]? — **meanders** = crooked lines [Hudson]? circles [Knight]? winding paths [Rolfe]? — The windings of the ancient river Meander are said to be due largely to its shifting its channel as it strolls through the sandy flats. —

Alonso. Old lord, I cannot blame thee,
Who am myself attach'd with weariness,
To the dulling of my spirits; sit down, and rest.
Even here I will put off my hope, and keep it
No longer for my flatterer; he is drown'd
Whom thus we stray to find, and the sea mocks
Our frustrate search on land. Well, let him go. 10
    Antonio. [*Aside to Sebastian*] I am right glad that he's
        so out of hope.
Do not, for one repulse, forego the purpose
That you resolv'd to effect.
    Sebastian. [*Aside to Antonio*] The next advantage
Will we take throughly.
    Antonio. [*Aside to Sebastian*] Let it be to-night;
For, now they are oppress'd with travel, they
Will not, nor cannot, use such vigilance
As when they are fresh.
    Sebastian. [*Aside to Antonio*] I say, to-night; no more.
            [*Solemn and strange music.*
    Alonso. What harmony is this? — My good friends, hark!
    Gonzalo. Marvellous sweet music!

Enter PROSPERO *above, invisible. Enter several strange Shapes, bringing in a banquet: they dance about it with gentle actions of salutation; and, inviting the King, etc., to eat, they depart.*

    Alonso. Give us kind keepers, heavens! — What were these?
    Sebastian. A living drollery. Now I will believe 21

---

5. **attach'd.** Fr. *attacher*, doublet of *attaquer*. Littré suggests a connection with Gæl. *tac*, a nail. *Brachet.* "The regular O. F. sense was to 'fasten,' as in Mod. Eng. . . . The earlier Eng. sense of 'arrest, seize' arose . . . as an elliptical expression for '*attach* by some tie to the control or jurisdiction of the court,' i.e. so that it shall have a *hold*. . . . The Ital. equivalent is *attaccare*. . . . *Attaccare battaglia*, to *join* battle, *attaccarsi a*, to fasten (one's self) upon, 'attack.'" Murray's *New Eng. Dict.* — Shakes. uses 'attach' repeatedly in the sense of *seize*. — 8. **no longer for** = ᴜo longer to be? — 10. **frustrate.** Shakes. often avoids adding -*d* or -*ed* after the sound of *d* or *t*. Abbott, 341, 342. — 12. **forego** = quit, give up? — Would *forgo* be better? — The *for* (not *fore*) = from, forth, away? — See note on *fordo* in our *Hamlet*, V, i, 210. — 14. **throughly** = thoroughly? *Mer. of Ven.*, II, vii, 42; IV, i, 164. — 21. **drollery** = puppet-show. Here the figures are living. — Fr. *drôle*, a knave, sharp rogue;

That there are unicorns; that in Arabia
There is one tree, the phœnix' throne, one phœnix
At this hour reigning there.
　Antonio.　　　　　　I'll believe both;
And what does else want credit, come to me,
And I'll be sworn 'tis true; travellers ne'er did lie,
Though fools at home condemn 'em.
　Gonzalo.　　　　　　　　If in Naples
I should report this now, would they believe me?
If I should say I saw such islanders, —
For, certes, these are people of the island, —　　　　30
Who, though they are of monstrous shape, yet, note,
Their manners are more gentle-kind than of
Our human generation you shall find
Many, nay, almost any.
　Prospero. [*Aside*]　　Honest lord,
Thou hast said well; for some of you there present
Are worse than devils.
　Alonso.　　　　　　I cannot too much muse
Such shapes, such gesture, and such sound, expressing —
Although they want the use of tongue — a kind
Of excellent dumb discourse.

---

drole, a wag; Icel. *troll*, a hobgoblin. *Skeat.*— 22. **unicorns.** Poetically evolved from the rhinoceros?— Lat. *unus*, one; *cornu*, horn. — 23. **phœnix.** Herodotus, in *Euterpe*, ii, 73, and Pliny, Lib. X, ii, describe this bird. Herodotus tells us it "makes its appearance . . . only once in 500 years. . . . They say that it comes on the death of its sire. If he is like the picture . . . the plumage of his wings is partly golden-colored and partly red; in outline and size he is very like an eagle." Pliny quotes the noble Roman senator Mamilius as saying that the phœnix " liveth 660 years, and when he groweth old, and begins to decay, he builds himself with the twigs and branches of the canell or cinnamon and frankincense trees; and when he hath filled it up with all sorts of sweet aromatical spices, yieldeth up his life thereupon. . . . It was assured unto me that the said bird died with that tree [date-tree, called in Greek φοίνιξ, phoinix], and revived of itself again." *Holland's translation*, 1601. — It was commonly said that the bird was consumed in flames, and from the ashes sprang a new phœnix. Hence the name in *fire-insurance*. See Shakespeare's *Phœnix and the Turtle*, Milton's *Samson Agonistes*, and Moore's *Paradise and the Peri.*— 30. **certes.** Used by Shakes. 5 times, says Rolfe.— 31. **who.** This use of *who*, without a verb, is a Latin idiom, and illustrates what has been called the *nominativus pendens*. See our *Mer. of Ven.*, I, iii, 126, note on 'Who, if he break.' — 36. **muse** = wonder [Keightley]? wonder at [Wright, Hudson, Rolfe; etc.]?— Keightley puts a pause after 'muse,' and makes a broken sentence of what follows. — Lat. *mussare*, to mutter, grumble; brood over [Phillpotts]?— O. Fr. *muse*, mouth, akin to *muzzle*; Ital. *muso*, snout, face. The image is that of a dog snuffling idly about, and musing which direction to take!

Prospero. [*Aside*] Praise in departing.
Francisco. They vanish'd strangely.
Sebastian. No matter, since 40
They have left their viands behind; for we have stomachs—
Will't please you taste of what is here?
Alonzo. Not I.
Gonzalo. Faith, sir, you need not fear. When we were boys,
Who would believe that there were mountaineers
Dew-lapp'd like bulls, whose throats had hanging at 'em
Wallets of flesh? or that there were such men
Whose heads stood in their breasts? which now we find
Each putter-out of five for one will bring us
Good warrant of.
Alonso. I will stand to and feed,
Although my last; no matter, since I feel 50
The best is past.—Brother, my lord the duke,
Stand to, and do as we.

Thunder and lightning. Enter ARIEL, *like a harpy; claps his wings upon the table, and with a quaint device the banquet vanishes.*

Skeat.—39. **Praise in departing** = do not praise too soon?—Proverbial?—45. **dew-lapp'd**, etc. Swiss victims of *goitre*, tumor on the throat [Lat. *guttur*, throat; Fr. *goître*]?—See our *Mid. N. Dr.*, IV, i, 119.—46. **wallets**, etc. "It is not difficult to surmise that the pouched apes gave rise to the story." *Furness.*—47. **heads stood in their breasts.** So Pliny, *Nat. Hist.*, v, 8; Hakluyt's *Voyages* (1598); Othello, I, iii, 144.—48. **putter-out** = one who puts to sea [Schmidt]? investor, depositor?—**putter-out of five** = putter-out at the rate of five [Wright, Collier, Knight, etc.]?—'A popular mode of adventurous betting.'—"I intend to travel.... I will put forth some £5,000, to be paid me 5 for 1, upon the return of my wife, myself, and my dog from the Turk's court in Constantinople. If all or either of us miscarry in the journey, 'tis gone; if we be successful, why there will be £25,000." Ben Jonson's *Every Man Out of His Humor.*

Stage direction. *Enter Ariel as a harpy*, etc.—If a doubt could ever be entertained whether Shakespeare was a great poet, acting upon laws arising out of his own nature, and not without law, as has been sometimes idly asserted, that doubt must be removed by the character of Ariel. The very first words uttered by this being introduce the spirit, not as an angel, above man; not as a gnome, or a fiend, below man; but while the poet gives him the faculties and the advantages of reason, he divests him of all mortal character, not positively, it is true, but negatively. In air he lives, from air he derives his being, in air he acts; and all his colors and properties seem to have been obtained from the rainbow and the skies.—Coleridge's *Seven Lectures.*

Ariel. You are three men of sin, whom destiny,
That hath to instrument this lower world
And what is in't, the never-surfeited sea
Hath caus'd to belch up — *you!* — and on this island,
Where man doth not inhabit, you 'mongst men
Being most unfit to live. I have made you mad;
And even with such-like valor men hang and drown
Their proper selves.
   [*Alonso, Sebastian, and Antonio draw their swords.*
      You fools! I and my fellows 60
Are ministers of Fate; the elements,
Of whom your swords are temper'd, may as well
Wound the loud winds, or with bemock'd-at stabs
Kill the still-closing waters, as diminish
One dowle that's in my plume. My fellow-ministers
Are like invulnerable. If you could hurt,
Your swords are now too massy for your strengths,
And will not be uplifted. But remember, —

---

52. Ariel in the character of a harpy, and the banquet scene, are imitated from Vergil's *Æneid*, iii, 209 *et seq.* — **men of sin.** Biblical? 2 *Thess.*, ii, 3. — 53. **to instrument.** II, i, 73. — 54. **never-surfeited**, etc. The sea, that swallows all, cannot contain in its maw these three rascals, but vomits them forth! — 55. **to belch up — you! — and.** Here we deviate from the usual punctuation and interpretation. The common reading is, 'Hath caused to belch up you; and '; the common interpretation makes ' you ' redundant, thus: "*whom* destiny hath caused the never-surfeited sea to belch up *you.*" Abbott (249), Collier, Wright, Hudson and others declare the 'you' to be supplementary, superfluous, or even 'extremely awkward.' Staunton and Hudson would change 'you' to 'yea.' But suppose we adopt a different punctuation. Remember that three men, Alonzo, Sebastian, and Antonio, are to be singled out. They naturally are together, slightly apart from Gonzalo, Adrian, Francisco, and the others. At the words 'belch up,' the three naturally turn to glance at the rest, all of whom have been cast up by the nauseated sea. By a gesture, a look, a pause, and an intensely emphatic YOU, Ariel separates these three great sinners from the rest of the company, and notifies them that they alone are the 'vessels of wrath fitted to destruction.' *Rom.*, ix, 22. Does not our explanation give dramatic vividness and energy to the otherwise bungling, tame, and feeble utterance? — 59. **such-like.** The critics pronounce this pleonastic, because *such* is itself shortened from A. S. *swulc, suilc, suilch,* or *sich,* or Gothic *swa,* so; and A. S. *lik,* Gothic *leiks,* like. *Abbott,* 278. — 60. **proper** = appropriate? own? — 62. **whom.** *Abbott,* 264. — 63. See the somewhat similar passage in *Macb.*, V, viii, 9, 10. — 64. **still-closing.** I, ii, 229. — 65. **dowle** = filament of a feather or of down? — Skeat makes *down* akin to *dust,* meaning that which is blown. Wright and others show *down* and *dowle* to be equivalent. — 66. **like** = similarly? alike? — 67. **massy** = bulky? heavy? massive? — Gr. μάσσειν, massein, to knead; μαζα, maza, Lat. *massa,* a kneaded lump, dough; barley bread; Fr. *masse,* mass, lump. — **strengths.** So *wraths,*

For that's my business to you, — that you three,
From Milan did supplant good Prospero,   70
Expos'd unto the sea, which hath requit it,
Him and his innocent child; for which foul deed
The Powers, delaying, not forgetting, have
Incens'd the seas and shores, yea, all the creatures,
Against your peace. Thee of thy son, Alonso,
They have bereft, and do pronounce by me,
Lingering perdition — worse than any death
Can be at once — shall step by step attend
You and your ways; whose wraths to guard you from, —
Which here, in this most desolate isle, else falls   80
Upon your heads, — is nothing but heart's sorrow,
And a clear life ensuing.

He vanishes in thunder; then, to soft music, enter the Shapes again, and dance with mocks and mows, and carry out the table.

    Prospero. [*Aside*] Bravely the figure of this harpy hast thou
Perform'd, my Ariel; a grace it had, devouring.
Of my instruction hast thou nothing bated
In what thou hadst to say; so, with good life

---

line 79. See on *lover*, our ed. of *Hamlet*, I, i, 173; *Jul. Cæs.*, I, ii, 39. Does the plural form indicate nicer discrimination? — 70. **supplant.** See on III, ii, 46. — 71. **requit.** See on *frustrate*, line 10; I, ii, 148; *Abbott*, 341, 342. — 73. **Powers,** that 'make for righteousness.' So "They fought from heaven; the stars in their courses fought against Sisera," *Judges*, v, 20; *Rom.*, ix, 22; *Luke*, xviii, 7; *Ecclesiastes*, viii, 11. — 78. **at once.** 'Death at once' vs. 'lingering perdition'? — 79, 80. **wraths . . . falls.** Explain the 'singular.' Is 'wraths' capable of being taken as *one?* — **which.** 'Singular' by attraction to the 'singular' substantive 'isle' [Wright]? — *Abbott*, 247, 333, 412. — 82. **clear.** *Macb.*, I, vii, 18. — " Ariel seems to me to represent the keenest perceiving intellect, separate from all moral consciousness and sense of responsibility. His power and knowledge are in some respects greater than those of his master, — he can do what Prospero cannot, — he lashes up the Tempest round the island, — he saves the king and his companions from the shipwreck, — he defeats the conspiracy of Sebastian and Antonio, and discovers the clumsy plot of the beast Caliban, — he wields immediate influence over the elements, and comprehends alike without indignation or sympathy, — which are moral results, — the sin and suffering of humanity. Therefore, — because he is only a spirit of knowledge, he is subject to the spirit of love." — *Mrs. F. A. Kemble*, quoted by Furness.
    82. **mows.** II, ii, 9. — 83. **bravely.** III, ii, 99. — 84. **devouring** = swallowing the banquet [Deighton]? absorbing [Schmidt]? appearing to devour [Dyce]? — 86. **with good life** = with all the truth of life itself,

And observation strange, my meaner ministers
Their several kinds have done. My high charms work,
And these mine enemies are all knit up
In their distractions: they now are in my power; 90
And in these fits I leave them, while I visit
Young Ferdinand,—whom they suppose is drown'd,—
And his and mine lov'd darling. [*Exit above.*

Gonzalo. I' the name of something holy, sir, why stand you
In this strange stare?
 Alonso. O, it is monstrous, monstrous!
Methought the billows spoke, and told me of it;
The winds did sing it to me, and the thunder,
That deep and dreadful organ-pipe, pronounc'd
The name of Prosper: it did bass my trespass.
Therefore my son i' the ooze is bedded; and 100
I'll seek him deeper than e'er plummet sounded,
And with him there lie mudded. [*Exit.*
 Sebastian. But one fiend at a time,
I'll fight their legions o'er.
 Antonio. I'll be thy second.
 [*Exeunt Sebastian and Antonio.*
 Gonzalo. All three of them are desperate; their great guilt,
Like poison given to work a great time after,
Now gins to bite the spirits.— I do beseech you

---

and with rare observance of the proprieties of action [Hudson, Wright]? good spirit [Rolfe]? 'With good life' is still proverbial in the west of England, and signifies *with the full bent or energy of the mind.* Henley. "So we say, 'he acted to the *life.*'" Johnson.—87. **meaner** = of lower rank?—Lat. *medianus, medius,* Fr. *moyen,* mean, middle, intermediate. —88. **several.** As in III, i, 42?—**kinds have done** = have acted out their several natures, i.e. their *parts* [Hudson]? acted out their characters [Meiklejohn]? The clown that brings the fatal asp to Cleopatra cautions her by saying, "The worm will do his kind." *Ant. and Cleop.,* V, ii, 261. —92. **whom . . . is drowned.** Confusion of two constructions, "who they suppose *is* drowned," "whom they suppose to *be* drowned"? *Abbott,* 410. More liberty than now in Shakespeare's day; thus: "Whom do men say that I, the Son of Man, am?" *Matt.,* xvi, 13. Even now, perhaps, the majority would take the same liberty.—93. **his and mine.** *Abbott,* 238.—99. **bass my trespass** = told in deep bass tones the story of my crime?—*Macb.,* III, iv, 122–126.—100. **Therefore** = that is the true reason why?—Emphatic?—102. **mudded.** "Any noun or adjective could be converted into a verb by the Elizabethan authors." *Abbott,* 290.
 But one = If there be but one? Let there be but one?—105. **poison,** etc. Such poisons, according to Holt (1749), and Steevens (1793), were

SCENE III.]   THE TEMPEST.   99

 That are of suppler joints, follow them swiftly,
And hinder them from what this ecstasy
May now provoke them to.
  Adrian.   Follow, I pray you. [*Exeunt.*

---

believed to be prepared in Africa. — 108. **ecstasy.** Gr. ἐκ, ek, out, στάσις, stasis, standing. The word is metaphoric, signifying the state of one 'out of his head.' See our *Hamlet*, II, i, 102.
 How much, if anything, of Shakespeare's religious belief may fairly be inferred from this remarkable scene?

ACT IV.

Scene I. *Before Prospero's Cell.*

Enter Prospero, Ferdinand, *and* Miranda.

Prospero. If I have too austerely punish'd you,
Your compensation makes amends, for I
Have given you here a third of mine own life,
Or that for which I live; who once again
I tender to thy hand. All thy vexations
Were but my trials of thy love, and thou
Hast strangely stood the test; here, afore heaven,
I ratify this my rich gift. O Ferdinand,
Do not smile at me that I boast her of,

ACT IV. Scene I. **3. third.** So the folios. But why *third?* How make a three-fold division of his 'life'? Holt supposes Prospero and Miranda to be two thirds, and Ferdinand the remaining third. Capell (Furness concurring) thinks the realm, the daughter, and the father constitute the three thirds of the 'life.' E. Magnusson (*Athenæum*, July 26, 1884) is quoted by Furness to this effect: "His life's triunity had, once upon a time, consisted of his now departed wife, his child, and himself," but Magnusson now concurs with Capell. Theobald, in March, 1728, suggested that the true reading was *thrid*, for third, and that what was meant was *thread*. Most subsequent editors have printed *thread;* Tollett, the Globe ed., Wright, and Phillpotts read *thrid;* Heath, *the thread:* Bailey, *the end.* To us, 'a thread,' however classic and suggestive of the three fatal spinners, seems a *feeble* utterance for one who is in a mood to *magnify* his gift to Ferdinand. Any one of a dozen children would be a *thread.* Guessing "is the word: it is a deed in fashion"! Shakespeare had perhaps read in the *Carmen Nuptiale* of Catullus, *Virginitas non tota tua est: ex parte parentum est: Tertia pars patri data, pars data tertia matri, Tertia sola tua est,* Maidenhood is not all thine: it partly belongs to thy parents; a third part given to father, a third part to mother, a third is thine alone. Here are three, Prospero, Miranda, Ferdinand: they shall share equally in her who is 'my life.' For twelve years or more (see I, ii, 16, 17, and *King John*, III, iv, 104) that 'life' had belonged to *two*, father and daughter; now it shall be parted among *three.* — Shakes. may combine several meanings in this 'third.'—**7. afore.** *Rom.*, ix, 23.—9. **boast her of** = boast of her?— Keightley reads *boast of her,* and Furness approves. We follow the 1st folio. All the other folios and all the editors read *boust her off;* a reading, says Furness, "which somehow carries with it the image of an auctioneer's exaggeration and volubility, which is, as Sydney Smith would say, 'infinitely distress-

For thou shalt find she will outstrip all praise, 10
And make it halt behind her.
   Ferdinand.   I do believe it
Against an oracle.
   Prospero. Then, as my gift and thine own acquisition
Worthily purchas'd, take my daughter: but
If thou dost break her virgin-knot before
All sanctimonious ceremonies may
With full and holy rite be minister'd,
No sweet aspersion shall the heavens let fall
To make this contract grow; but barren hate,
Sour-eyed disdain, and discord shall bestrew 20
The union — with weeds so loathly
That you shall hate it both: therefore take heed,
As Hymen's lamps shall light you.
   Ferdinand.   As I hope
For quiet days, fair issue, and long life,
With such love as 'tis now, the strong'st suggestion
Our worser genius can, shall never melt
Mine honor into lust, to take away

---

ing.'"—11. **halt.** *Mer. of Ven.*, III, ii, 129; *Wint. T.*, V, iii, 52, 53.—13. **gift.** The folios have *guest*. Rowe (1709) and all subsequent editors read *gift*. Any good reason for retaining *guest*?—15. **virgin-knot** = maiden zone or belt. This girdle was unclasped by the husband at the wedding. Prospero's care! He is both father and mother to her; she so young, motherless, and loving, like Mildred in Browning's *Blot in the 'Scutcheon*, II, 361, 362.—16. **sanctimonious.** Whence originates the modern unfavorable sense?—18. **aspersion.** Lat. *ad*, to; *spargĕre*, to scatter; *aspergĕre*, to sprinkle; *aspersio*, sprinkling. Any allusion to sprinkling with 'holy water'?—Whence the present ill use of the word?—21. **The union of your bed with weeds so loathly**, etc. Is this the order of ideas: shall bestrew the union of your bed with so loathly [i.e. disgusting, loathsome] weeds?—22. **That you shall hate it both** = that both of you shall hate it?—23. **Hymen's lamps.** Elze shows that 'lamps' of the folio should be 'lamp.' See line 97. Furness approves the correction. It seems, however, to be unimportant.—Hymen was the handsome youthful god of the marriage ceremony, not of married life. He is son of Apollo, carries in his hand a bridal torch. See in our *Masterpieces*, note, p. 78.—25. **as 'tis now, the murkiest den.** A. S. *murc*, dark; related to μέλας, melas, black.—26. **The most opportune place, the strong'st**, etc. Shakes. twice uses *opportune*. He accents the 2d syl.—27. **worser.** Used by Shakes. 17 times.—*Abbott*, 11.—**genius.** Shakes. seems to recognize two 'geniuses,' a guardian angel, and an evil tempter. "In mediæval theology, the rational soul is an angel, the lowest in the hierarchy for being clothed for a time in the perishing vesture of the body. But it is not necessarily an angel of light." *Edinburgh Review*, July, 1869, p. 98.—See our ed. of *Jul. Cæs.*, II, i, 66; our *Macb.*, III, i, 55. —**can.** Ellipsis? *Hamlet*, IV, vii, 83; *Abbott*, 307.—**melt.** *Timon of A.*, IV, iii, 365—367.—28. **lust, to take away.** Supply 'so as' before 'to

The edge of that day's celebration
When I shall think, or Phœbus' steeds are founder'd, 30
Or night kept chain'd below.
   Prospero.   Fairly spoke.
Sit then and talk with her; she is thine own.—
What, Ariel! my industrious servant, Ariel!

             Enter ARIEL.

   Ariel. What would my potent master? here I am.
   Prospero. Thou and thy meaner fellows your last service
Did worthily perform, and I must use you
In such another trick. Go bring the rabble,
O'er whom I give thee power, here to this place.
Incite them to quick motion, for I must
Bestow upon the eyes of this young couple 40
Some vanity of mine art; it is my promise,
And they expect it from me.
   Ariel.   Presently?
   Prospero. Ay, with a twink.
   Ariel.   Before you can say 'come' and 'go,'
          And breathe twice, and cry 'so, so,'
          Each one, tripping on his toe,
          Will be here with mop and mow.—
          Do you love me, master? no?
   Prospero. Dearly, my delicate Ariel. Do not approach
Till thou dost hear me call.
   Ariel.   Well, I conceive.   [*Exit.*

---

take'?—29. **The edge of that day's celebration** = the keen enjoyment of the celebration of our wedding-day [Jephson]? The *-ion* in celebration is resolved in scanning into two syllables.—30. **or** = either?— **Phœbus'** = the sun-god's. See our *Hamlet*, III, ii, 138.—**founder'd.** "The signe to know it [foundering of horses] is, the horse cannot go, but will stand cripling with al his foure legs together." Topsell's *Hist. of Foure-footed Beasts*, 1608, quoted by Furness.—31. **chained.** As the sun's chariot goes down in the west, night's car ascends in the east; both so slowly that it seems as if the evening's festivities would never come.— **spoke.** Abbott, 338.—37. **rabble** = lower spirits? Stephano, Trinculo, etc.?—"Not used slightingly." Furness.—O. Du. *rabbelen*, to chatter. Gr. ραβάσσειν, rabassein, to make a noise. The suffix *-le* gives a frequentative force. *Skeat.*—41. **vanity** = illusion [Steevens]? *Psalms*, xxxix, 6; *Ecclesiastes*, xii, 8.—42. **presently.** I, ii, 125.—43. **twink** = twinkling?—A. S. *twiccan*, to twitch; *twinclian*, to twinkle; *twink* is nasalized from *twiccian*. *Skeat.*—47. **mop.** Du. *moppen*, Local Ger. *muffen*, to sulk; Eng. *mop* and *mope*, to grimace.—**mow.** III, iii, 82; II, ii, 9.—

Prospero. Look thou be true; do not give dalliance 51
Too much the rein: the strongest oaths are straw
To the fire i' the blood.
 Ferdinand.   I warrant you, sir;
The white cold virgin snow upon my heart—
 Prospero.   Well.—
Now come, my Ariel! bring a corollary,
Rather than want a spirit; appear, and pertly!—
No tongue! all eyes! be silent. [*Soft music.*

Enter IRIS.

 Iris. Ceres, most bounteous lady, thy rich leas 60
Of wheat, rye, barley, vetches, oats, and pease;
Thy turfy mountains, where live nibbling sheep,
And flat meads thatch'd with stover, them to keep;
Thy banks with pioned and twilled brims,

---

51. **dalliance.** A. S. *dol*, foolish; Du. *dwalen*, to be foolish.—52. **rein.** Lat. *re*, back, *tenēre*, to hold; *retinēre*, to hold back; *retinaculum*, a holdback, tether, halter, rein. Fr. *rêne*, bridle strap, rein. *Skeat, Brachet.*—53. **To the fire i' the blood; be more abstemious.** *To the fire*, etc. So we speak of 'fetters of flax to bind the flame.' *Abstemious*, Skeat derives fr. Lat. *abs*, from, and obsolete *temum*, strong drink. — 54. **Or else good night your vow!** Lines 23–28.—55. **The white cold virgin snow.** Shakespeare is fond of this imagery. *Coriolanus*, V, iii, 64–67.—56. **Abates the ardor of my liver.** Capell cites from Elyot's *Castle of Health*, 1610, the converse, "that the heat of the heart may vanquish the colde of the liver." — The liver was the supposed seat of the passions, particularly love. *As You L. I.*, III, ii, 390; *Mer. of Ven.*, I, i, 81. — 57. **corollary** = supernumerary, surplus, an extra. Gr. κορώνη, *korone*, curved end of a bow; Welsh *crwn*, round; Lat. *corona*, garland, crown; *corolla*, little crown; *corollarium*, gift of a garland *besides* the regular pay; a gratuity; the gift of an actor in addition to his wages. *Worc., Brachet*, etc.—58. **want.** Emphatic?—58. **pertly.** W. *pert*, smart, spruce.—59. **silent.** In the presence of supernatural beings in *Shakes.*, silence is enjoined. IV, i, 124–127; *Macb.*, IV, i, 70, "Hear his speech, but say thou nought." — "Prospero surrounds the marriage of Ferdinand to his daughter with a religious awe. Ferdinand must honor her as sacred, and win her by hard toil. But the work of the higher imagination is not drudgery — it is swift and serviceable among all the elements — fire upon the topmast, the sea-nymphs upon the sands, Ceres, the goddess of earth, with harvest blessings, in the Masque. — It is essentially Ariel, an airy spirit — the imaginative genius of poetry, but recently delivered in England from long slavery to Sycorax." — *Edward Dowden.*
60. **leas.** A. S. *leah*, field.—61. **vetches.** Leguminous plants. In folio *fetches*, still pronounced so in portions of England; the *fetches* of *Isaiah*, xxviii, 25, 27; *Ezek.*, iv, 9.—63. **stover.** Coarse winter fodder for cattle? O. Fr. *estover*, necessaries, provisions; akin probably to *stow*, or to Lat. *stare*, to stand?—64. **pioned and twilled brims.** Of these four

Which spongy April at thy hest betrims,
To make cold nymphs chaste crowns; and thy broom groves,
Whose shadow the dismissed bachelor loves,
Being lass-lorn; thy pole-clipt vineyard;
And thy sea-marge, sterile and rocky-hard,
Where thou thyself dost air; — the queen o' the sky, 70
Whose watery arch and messenger am I,
Bids thee leave these, and with her sovereign grace,
Here on this grass-plot, in this very place,
To come and sport. Her peacocks fly amain;
Approach, rich Ceres, her to entertain.

---

words the innumerable emendations and explanations are 'tedious as a king,' 'most tolerable and not to be endured,' to use Dogberry's happy phrases. See the *Var. Ed.* of Furness, who says, "We have simply lost the meaning of words which were perfectly intelligible to Shakespeare's audience. As agricultural or horticultural terms, 'pioned' and 'twilled' will be some day, probably, sufficiently explained to enable us to weave from them the chaste crowns for cold nymphs." With Hudson, Phillpotts, and Deighton, we have felt inclined to adopt Dr. T. S. Baynes's explanation in the *Edinburgh Review*, of October, 1872, confirmed as it seemed to be by our own observation at Stratford in 1882, as follows: "Twilled is the very word to describe the crowded sedges in the shallower reaches of the Avon as it winds around Stratford. It was, indeed, while watching the masses of waving sedge cutting the water line of the Avon, not far from Stratford Church, that we first felt the peculiar force and significance of the epithet. And although the season was too far advanced for the reeds to be brightened by the flowers of the marsh marygold [called *peony* by the Warwickshire peasantry], the plant was abundant enough to glorify the banks in the early spring. The whole line, therefore, gives a vivid and truthful picture of what is most characteristic of water margins at that period of the year." Thus far Baynes; but able botanists deny his conclusions. See *Furness.*—line 129; *Lycidas*, 104.—65. **spongy** = full of moisture as a wet sponge?—66. **broom groves** = woods overgrown with genista, pathless woods [Schmidt]?—67. See on *bachelerie* in our *Masterpieces*, p. 27.—68. **lass-lorn**. *Lass*, fem. of *lad*, shortened fr. *laddess!* The *-ess* is for *-es*, which is a Welsh fem. ending. *Lorn* (*lo-ren*) is old past part. of *lose*. *Skeat.* — **pole-clipt** = clipped as with shears so as to be trained to poles [Jephson, Delius]? with vines twined about the poles, embracing the poles [Wright, Phillpotts]? with poles clipped or twined about, embraced, clasped, by vines [Steevens, Dyce, Hudson, Meiklejohn]?—A. S. *clyppan*, to embrace; Icel. *klippa*, to cut, shear the hair. The orig. sense was to draw tightly together. *Skeat.* — **vineyard**. Trisyl.?—69. **sea-marge**. A. S. *meark*, mark; akin to Lat. *margo*, margin.—71. **Juno's messenger** identifies herself with the rainbow? Says Hartley Coleridge, "Shakespeare manifestly turns the heathen deities into the elementary powers, resolving Greek anthropomorphism into its first principles. Ceres is the earth."—73. **to come**. Like *to suffer*, III, i, 62?—74. **peacocks** draw Juno's car?—**amain**. A. S. *on*, (later) *a i.* (latest) *a* = in, with. A. S. *mayen*, strength. II, i, 180. 'Might' and 'main,' like 'mop' and 'mow,' are almost, if not quite, exact equivalents.

Enter CERES.

Ceres. Hail, many-color'd messenger, that ne'er
Dost disobey the wife of Jupiter;
Who, with thy saffron wings, upon my flowers
Diffusest honey-drops, refreshing showers,
And with each end of thy blue bow dost crown   80
My bosky acres and my unshrubb'd down,
Rich scarf to my proud earth! Why hath thy queen
Summon'd me hither, to this short-grass'd green?
    Iris. A contract of true love to celebrate,
And some donation freely to estate
On the blest lovers.
    Ceres.   Tell me, heavenly bow,
If Venus or her son, as thou dost know,
Do now attend the queen? Since they did plot
The means that dusky Dis my daughter got,
Her and her blind boy's scandal'd company   90
I have forsworn.
    Iris.   Of her society
Be not afraid; I met her deity
Cutting the clouds towards Paphos, and her son
Dove-drawn with her. Here thought they to have done
Some wanton charm upon this man and maid,
Whose vows are, that no bed-right shall be paid
Till Hymen's torch be lighted: but in vain;
Mars's hot minion is return'd again;
Her waspish-headed son has broke his arrows,

---

78. **saffron.** Vergil's *Æneid*, iv, 700, seems in Shakespeare's mind. — 81. **bosky.** Ital. *bosco*, busk; fr. Mid. Lat. *boscus*, a wood. Milton has 'bosky bourn,' i.e. woody bourn. — **down** = large open plain? sandy hill? — A.S. *dún*. — 85. **estate** = settle? endow? — Fr. *état*, fr. Lat. *status*, state. — 89. **that ... got,** etc. = which obtained my daughter for Dis? by which Dis obtained my daughter? — **Dis.** Lat. *dives*, rich. When S. wants a monosyl. for the name, '*Dis*' suffices; when a dissyl., 'Pluto.' The king of the realm of shades is poetically characterized as 'dusky'; just as in Virgil, *atri Ditis*, of black Pluto, *Æneid*, vi, 127. — Milton has 'gloomy Dis' in *Par. Lost*, iv, 270. — 93. **Paphos.** Near Old Paphos on the west coast of Cyprus, sea-born Venus (Gr. Aphrodite) first floated ashore. S. has in mind *Æneid*, i, 415-417? — 94. **dove-drawn.** So usually represented. Horace makes her chariot to be drawn by swans. — 96. **vows are.** We should say 'vow is.' See III, iii, 79. — **that no,** etc. = there shall be no consummation of the union. — **Hymen's.** Line 23. — 98. **minion** = favorite. See our *Macb.*, I, ii, 19. Venus of course is

Swears he will shoot no more, but play with sparrows, 100
And be a boy right out.
   Ceres.   Highest queen of state,
Great Juno comes; I know her by her gait.

Enter JUNO.

Juno. How does my bounteous sister? Go with me
To bless this twain, that they may prosperous be,
And honor'd in their issue.   [*They sing.*

  Juno.   *Honor, riches, marriage, blessing!*
            Long continuance, and increasing
            Hourly joys be still upon you!
            Juno sings her blessings on you.
            Earth's increase, and foison plenty,   110
            Barns and garners never empty,
            Vines with clustering bunches growing,
            Plants with goodly burthen bowing;
            Spring come to you at the farthest
            In the very end of harvest!
            Scarcity and want shall shun you;
            Ceres' blessing so is on you.

  Ferdinand. This is a most majestic vision, and
Harmonious charmingly. May I be bold
To think these spirits?
  Prospero.   Spirits, which by mine art   120

---

meant. — 101. **right out** = outright? complete? — 102. **gait.** It was majestic. *Æneid*, i, 46, 405. Supernatural beings *glide*, not *walk!* *Par. Lost*, xii, 629, 630. "In gliding state she wins her easy way." Spoken of Venus in Gray's *Progress of Poesy*, 39. — 110. and **foison.** For *foison*, see II, i, 160. — The first folio omits *and*. Omitting *and*, Abbott would make a trisyl. of *in-cre-ease!* Allen, a dissyl. of *e-earth's!* Wright would make *earth's* into *earth-es*, as *moon* into *moon-es* in *Mid. N. Dr.*, II, i, 7. Says Furness, "Shakespeare always, I *think*, makes 'increase' an *iamb*. . . . Wherefore it seems to me that the simplest way is to accept the *and*." — *Psalms*, lxvii, 6. — Following the example of Theobald, all subsequent editors, except Holt and Furness, give lines 110–117 to Ceres. But the **stage direction,** *They sing*, would seem to imply that all three, Juno, Iris, and Ceres, *all sing.* — 114. **spring,** etc. *Levit.*, xxvi, 4, 5; *Amos*, ix, 13; *Faerie Q.*, III, vi, 42. So in the garden of Alcinous, *Odyssey*, vii, 115–125. — 119. **harmonious charmingly** charmingly harmonious [Hudson]? harmonious; charmingly! [Holt]? harmoniously charming [Steevens]? "Staunton with truth says that 'charmingly' here imports

I have from their confines call'd to enact
My present fancies.
   Ferdinand.   Let me live here ever·
So rare a wonder'd father and a wife
Makes this place Paradise.
   [*Juno and Ceres whisper, and send Iris on employment.*
   Prospero.   Sweet now, silence!
Juno and Ceres whisper seriously;
There's something else to do: hush, and be mute,
Or else our spell is marr'd.
   Iris. You nymphs, call'd Naiads, of the windring brooks,
With your sedg'd crowns and ever harmless looks,
Leave your crisp channels, and on this green land   130
Answer your summons; Juno does command.
Come, temperate nymphs, and help to celebrate
A contract of true love; be not too late. —

              Enter certain Nymphs.

You sunburnt sicklemen, of August weary,
Come hither from the furrow, and be merry.
Make holiday; your rye-straw hats put on,

---

magically, not delightfully." *Furness.* So Meiklejohn. — 121. **confines.** Lat. *con*, together; *finis*, boundary; Lat. *confines*, borders, boundaries. In *Hamlet*, I, i, 155, *confine* seems to mean bound which must not be passed, or place of confinement. — 123. **wise.** Some copies of folio 1 have 'wife,' and some 'wise.' The majority prefer 'wise.' White says, "To read 'wife' is to degrade the poetical feeling of the passage." So it is, if the passage merely means so wonderful a father *plus* a wife! On the other hand, if it means merely that Prospero is rarely wonderful and very wise! what a paradise! made up of a wonderful father and his wisdom! — Hudson suggests that we should 'extend the meaning' of 'so rare a wondered' (i.e. 'so rarely wonderful') to *wife*. So rarely wonderful a father and so rarely wonderful (and the word *Miranda* means to be wondered at) a wife! these in combination may well make a paradise for the young prince. Such extension of meaning is quite Shakespearian. — 237. **marr'd**, etc. Line 59. — 128. **Naiads** = fresh water nymphs? Gr. ναειν, naein, to flow. — **windring.** So the folios, 'wandering,' 'wand'-ring,' 'winding,' 'wiring,' have been suggested. Wright compares *wilderness* for 'wildness,' in *Meas. for Meas.*, III, i, 141. We might add *augurers* for 'augurs,' *Jul. Cæs.*, II, ii, 37. Is there not in *windring* a notion or feeling of intelligence on the part of the brooks, as if they, like persons, were directors of their own windings, and not simply passive? — 130. **crisp.** Milton has 'crisped brooks,' *Par. Lost*, iv, 237; and 'crisped shades,' *Comus*, 984. Lat. *crispus*, curled. The channel *looks* curled under the ripples

And these fresh nymphs encounter every one
In country footing.

Enter certain Reapers, properly habited: they join with the Nymphs in a graceful dance; towards the end whereof PROSPERO *starts suddenly, and speaks; after which, to a strange, hollow, and confused noise, they heavily vanish.*

Prospero. [*Aside*] I had forgot that foul conspiracy
Of the beast Caliban and his confederates   140
Against my life; the minute of their plot
Is almost come. — [*To the Spirits*] Well done! Avoid; no
 more!
Ferdinand. This is strange; your father's in some passion
That works him strongly.
Miranda.   Never till this day
Saw I him touch'd with anger so distemper'd.
Prospero. You do look, my son, in a mov'd sort,
As if you were dismay'd; be cheerful, sir.
Our revels now are ended. These our actors,
As I foretold you, were all spirits, and
Are melted into air, into thin air;   150
And, like the baseless fabric of this vision,
The cloud-capp'd towers, the gorgeous palaces,
The solemn temples, the great globe itself,
Yea, all which it inherit, shall dissolve,

---

through which the sunshine makes the lights and shadows wind and flit on the sandy bottom. — 138. **footing.** I, ii, 377.

142. **Avoid** = vacate (this place)? — Fr. *vider la maison.* — O. Fr. *avoider*, to empty: fr. Lat. *ex*, out; *viduare*, to empty. *Avoid* was the common phrase in bidding a spirit begone. — 145. **distemper'd.** *Hamlet*, III, ii, 280; *Abbott*, 439. — Why distempered? From the sense of all injuries, past and present, surging upon his mind at once [Phillpotts]? — 146. It is hard to believe that Shakes. wrote this line as it stands. Abbott's suggestion (483) is plausible, viz.: "Perhaps aware of Ferdinand's comment on his emotion, 'your father's in some passion,' Prospero turns to Ferdinand and says, 'it is *you* who are moved,' in

'Yóu | do lóok | my són | in a | mov'd sórt.'"

Might we not still further avoid the awkwardness by printing 'moved' in place of *mov'd*? thus:

"Yóu | do lóok | my són | in a móv | ed sort."

— **sort.** See II, i, 100; our *Jul. Cæs.*, I, ii, 201. — 149. **foretold.** Line 120. — 150. **into thin air.** A recollection of *in tenues auras*, into thin air, *Æneid*, ii, 791. — 154. **inherit.** Furness thinks it probable that *it* (mean-

SCENE I.] THE TEMPEST. 109

And, like this insubstantial pageant faded,
Leave not a rack behind. We are such stuff
As dreams are made on, and our little life
Is rounded with a sleep.—Sir, I am vex'd;
Bear with my weakness; my old brain is troubled.
Be not disturb'd with my infirmity: 160
If you be pleas'd, retire into my cell
And there repose; a turn or two I'll walk,
To still my beating mind.
    Ferdinand. Miranda. We wish your peace. [*Exeunt.*
Prospero. Come with a thought. I thank thee, Ariel: come!

Enter ARIEL.

Ariel. Thy thoughts I cleave to. What's thy pleasure?
Prospero.   · Spirit,
We must prepare to meet with Caliban.
    Ariel. Ay, my commander; when I presented Ceres,
I thought to have told thee of it, but I fear'd
Lest I might anger thee. 169

---

ing *globe*) is the subject, and *which* (meaning *which things*) the object, of *inherit*, the *s*, needed to convert 'inherit' into *inherits*, being present in the *s* of the succeeding 'shall.' Test!—II, ii, 162.—155. **pageant** = great and splendid show? Our *Mer. of Ven.*, I, i, 11; Furness's *The Tempest*, p. 212.—156. **rack** = scudding or drifting clouds? Icel. *rek*, drift, motion; *sky rek*, drifting clouds. The orig. sense of *wreck* or *wrack* is 'that which is drifted or driven ashore.' Skeat. Our *Hamlet*, II, ii, 470. So in Moore's *Fire Worshippers*,

> "The day is lowering: stilly black
> Sleeps the grim wave, while heaven's rack,
> Dispersed and wild, 'twixt earth and sky
> Hangs like a shattered canopy."

Shakes. seems to anticipate the deductions of science. Langley, in his *The New Astronomy*, tells how universes come and go like clouds successively forming and dissolving. *Psalms*, cii, 25, 26; *2 Peter*, iii, 10; *Rev.*, xx, 11; xxi, 1.—157. **on.** I, ii, 87. "Something could be said in favor of its retaining its ordinary meaning of *upon*." *Furness.*—158. **rounded** = completed, finished off as with a crown [Wright] ? rounded off with (the sleep of death) [Hudson]?—"Our birth is but a sleep and a forgetting." Wordsworth.—*Nos petites vies sont les isles du sommeil.* Darmesteter. *Hamlet*, III, i, 60-82; *Jul. Cæs.*, V, iii, 24, 25; *Lear*, V, iii, 175; *Richard II*, III, ii, 160, 161.—This magnificent passage, lines 150-158, is sometimes absurdly quoted to prove Shakes. an atheist; e.g. by Birch, *Philosophy and Religion of Shakespeare*, 1848; Douglas Campbell, *Puritans in England, Holland, and America*, 1894; but see I, ii, 159; III, iii, 72-82.
    164. **with a thought.** "With a thought, seven of the eleven I paid." *1 Henry IV*, II, iv, 202, 203.—166. **meet with** = encounter, oppose [Hudson, Wright, Deighton]?—167. **presented** = represented, played?—

Prospero. Say again, where didst thou leave these varlets?
Ariel. I told you, sir, they were red-hot with drinking;
So full of valor that they smote the air
For breathing in their faces, beat the ground
For kissing of their feet, yet always bending
Towards their project. Then I beat my tabor,
At which, like unback'd colts, they prick'd their ears,
Advanc'd their eyelids, lifted up their noses
As they smelt music; so I charm'd their ears
That, calf-like, they my lowing follow'd through
Tooth'd briers, sharp furzes, pricking gorse, and thorns, 180
Which enter'd their frail shins: at last I left them
I' the filthy mantled pool beyond your cell,
There dancing up to the chins, that the foul lake
O'erstunk their feet.
Prospero.   This was well done, my bird.
Thy shape invisible retain thou still;
The trumpery in my house, go bring it hither,
For stale to catch these thieves.
Ariel.   I go, I go.   [*Exit.*
Prospero. A devil, a born devil, on whose nature
Nurture can never stick; on whom my pains,
Humanely taken, all, all lost, quite lost;   190
And as with age his body uglier grows,
So his mind cankers. I will plague them all,
Even to roaring. —

Enter ARIEL, *loaden with glistering apparel, etc.*

Come hang them on this line.

---

174. **kissing of.** I, ii, 100.—175. **tabor.** III, ii, 119.—176. **unback'd.** *Mer. of Ven.*, V, i, 71.—177. **advanc'd.** I, ii, 407.—180. **tooth'd** = dentate?—**furzes** = thorny evergreen with yellow flowers?—**gorse** = thick prickly shrub akin to furze?—182. **mantled** = scum-covered?— O. Fr. *mantel*, later *manteau*, a cloak; Lat. *mantellum*, a napkin; also, as a means of covering, a cloak. The orig. sense seems to be 'covering.' Compare A. S. *mentel*, a mantle. *Skeat.*—184. **bird.** 'Chick,' V, i, 317. —186. **trumpery.** Fr. *trompe*, a trumpet; *tromper*, to deceive; *tromperie*, craft, wily fraud. *Skeat.* The orig. sense was to play on the trump, or trumpet. *Littré. Tromper*, properly to play the horn, alluding to quacks and mountebanks. *Brachet.*—187. **stale** = decoy, snare?— A. S. *stalu*, theft; *stelan*, to steal. Probably 'steal' meant 'to put by.' *Skeat.* Autolycus, in *Winter's T.*, was 'a snapper-up of unconsidered trifles.'
193. **glistering.** Shakes. and Milton do not use *glisten.*—**line** = linden or lime-tree? clothes-line? The players used to stretch up a clothes-line on the stage; and Knight, Dyce, Staunton, and others think

PROSPERO *and* ARIEL *remain invisible. Enter* CALIBAN, STEPHANO, *and* TRINCULO, *all wet.*

Caliban. Pray you, tread softly, that the blind mole may not
Hear a foot fall; we now are near his cell.
Stephano. Monster, your fairy, which you say is a harmless fairy, has done little better than played the Jack with us.
Trinculo. Monster, I do smell all horse — at which
My nose is in great indignation.
Stephano. So is mine. — Do you hear, monster? If I should take a displeasure against you, look you, —
Trinculo. Thou wert but a lost monster. 200
Caliban. Good my lord, give me thy favor still.
Be patient, for the prize I'll bring thee to
Shall hoodwink this mischance; therefore speak softly.
All's hush'd as midnight yet.
Trinculo. Ay, but to lose our bottles in the pool, —
Stephano. There is not only disgrace and dishonor in that, monster, but an infinite loss.
Trinculo. That's more to me than my wetting; yet this is your harmless fairy, monster.
Stephano. I will fetch off my bottle, though I be o'er ears for my labor. 211
Caliban. Prithee, my king, be quiet. Seest thou here,
This is the mouth o' the cell; no noise, and enter.
Do that good mischief which may make this island
Thine own for ever, and I, thy Caliban,
For aye thy foot-licker.
Stephano. Give me thy hand. I do begin to have bloody thoughts.

---

they were right in so doing, while Hunter, Wright, Brae, Rolfe, insist that a line-tree is meant. The battle is still on, and, like Grant, they "will fight it out on this line if it takes all summer." — 194. **blind mole** = Prospero? ellipsis of even? — Moles were supposed blind, but with hearing preternaturally acute. — 197. **Jack** = jack o' lantern, will o' the wisp, *ignis fatuus* that leads into the bogs? the knave (with an allusion to cards)? II, ii, 6. — 201. **Good my lord.** In such expressions 'my lord' 'my liege,' etc., seem compound nouns, like Fr. *monsieur*, Du. *mynheer*. See our *Jul. Cæs.*, II, i, 255; our *Hamlet*, I, ii, 50. — Abbott, 484, thinks this 'good' a dissyl., as if Caliban had said *Goo-ood!* — 203. **hoodwink** = blindfold? conceal? impose upon? — See our *Hamlet*, III, iv, 64; our *Macbeth*, IV, iii, 72. — 215. I. Like 'I' in '*between you and I*,' *Mer. of Ven.*, III, ii, 313? or is *I* the subject of *will be*, understood? *Abbott*, 209. —

Trinculo. O King Stephano! O peer! O worthy Stephano! look what a wardrobe here is for thee! 220
Caliban. Let it alone, thou fool; it is but trash.
Trinculo. O, ho, monster! we know what belongs to a frippery.—O King Stephano!
Stephano. Put off that gown, Trinculo; by this hand! I'll have that gown.
Trinculo. Thy grace shall have it.
Caliban. The dropsy drown this fool! What do you mean,
To dote thus on such luggage? Let's alone,
And do the murther first; if he awake,
From toe to crown he'll fill our skins with pinches, 230
Make us strange stuff.
Stephano. Be you quiet, monster.—Mistress line, is not this my jerkin? Now is the jerkin under the line; now, jerkin, you are like to lose your hair, and prove a bald jerkin.
Trinculo. Do, do; we steal by line and level, an't like your grace.
Stephano. I thank thee for that jest; here's a garment for't: wit shall not go unrewarded while I am king of this country. 'Steal by line and level' is an excellent pass of pate; there's another garment for't. 240
Trinculo. Monster, come, put some lime upon your fingers, and away with the rest.

---

220. **wardrobe.** As will be seen by the version in Percy's *Reliques*, the 'wardrobe' is especially prominent in the old ballad beginning "King Stephen was a worthy peer."—221. **trash.** See note on I, ii, 81.—222. **frippery** = old-clothes shop?—Fr. *friper*, to crumple; **wear out**: devour; *fripe*, a rag, scrap; *friperie*, trifles, rags, 'old-clo'.'—224. **by this hand!** III, ii, 47.—228. **alone** = you and me without Trinculo. Beginning with Theobald, many editors read, "Let's along"; some, with Collier, "Let't alone"; Hanmer, 'Let it alone.'—232. **line.** See on this word in line 193.—233. **jerkin** = doublet? jacket?—Du. *jurk*, a frock.—234. **hair.** 'Crossing the line' [i.e. equator]? Sailors were liable to lose their hair from fever, or by tricks played on them. Much learning has been expended in explaining the puns of the drunken butler and the professional jester. Clothes-line, equinoctial line, plumb-line, hangman's line, and even hair line, as if the rope were made of *hair* (which a cockney would call '*air*, and Mr. Brae says clothes were hung out to be *aired*—*air line therefore*!)—each of these offers itself, or is pressed into service, "as who should say, 'And you will not have me, choose!'"—235. **by line and level**; i.e. scientifically?—239. **pass of pate** = thrust or sally of wit? *Pass* is a fencing term; *pate*, slang for 'head.' See our *Hamlet*, II, ii, 557.—241. **lime** = bird-lime. See on *limed*, in our *Hamlet*, III, iii, 68.—

Caliban. I will have none on't; we shall lose our time,
And all be turn'd to barnacles, or to apes
With foreheads villanous low.

Stephano. Monster, lay to your fingers; help to bear this away where my hogshead of wine is, or I'll turn you out of my kingdom: go to, carry this.

Trinculo. And this.

Stephano. Ay, and this.   250

A noise of hunters heard. Enters divers Spirits, in shape of dogs and hounds, and hunt them about, PROSPERO *and* ARIEL *setting them on.*

Prospero. Hey, Mountain, hey!

Ariel. Silver! there it goes, Silver!

Prospero. Fury, Fury! there, Tyrant, there! hark, hark!—
  [*Caliban, Stephano, and Trinculo are driven out.*
Go charge my goblins that they grind their joints,
With dry convulsions, shorten up their sinews
With aged cramps, and more pinch-spotted make them
Than pard or cat o' mountain.

Ariel.   Hark, they roar!

---

244. **barnacles** = shell-fish growing on timber in water? geese fabled to have been evolved from shell-fish growing on trees and falling into the water?—Max Müller (*Science of Lang.*, 2d series, Am. ed., p. 552 *et seq.*) thinks the word to be derived like 'Barney' from *Hibernia*, Ireland! Rolfe quotes from Marston's *Malcontent*, III, i,

  "Be like your Scotch barnacle, now a block,
  Instantly a worm, and presently a great goose."

In Butler's *Hudibras*, we read

  "As barnacles turn Soland geese
  In th' islands of the Orcades."

—Barnacles or geese? that's the question!—245. **foreheads,** etc. Is it clear that Shakes. liked high foreheads? *Two Gent. of Ven.,* IV, iv, 186; *Ant. and Cleop.,* III, iii, 36, 37; Chaucer's *Prol.,* 154, 155; *Faerie Q.,* II, iii, 34.—**villanous.** In Shakes. adjectives are freely used as adverbs. Abbott, 1.—248. **go to** = hush up? come? go to ——?—Our *Mer. of Ven.,* I, iii, 105.—254. **grind their joints with dry,** etc. "The mucilage sometimes gets dried out of the joints . . . so as to cause a creaking or grating sound. . . . Of course the effect is very painful." Hudson.—255. **aged** = huge [Hudson]? such as afflict the old [Wright, Deighton, etc.]?—I, ii, 367.—256. **pard** = panther? Leopard (leo-pard) is lion pard. See our *As You Like It,* II, vii, 150.—**cat o' mountain** = catamount? wild

THE TEMPEST. [ACT IV. SCENE I.

Prospero. Let them be hunted soundly. At this hour
Lies at my mercy all mine enemies;
Shortly shall all my labors end, and thou   260
Shalt have the air at freedom. For a little
Follow, and do me service.   [*Exeunt.*

---

cat? ounce? puma? — *Mid. N. Dr.*, II, ii, 30. — 259. **lies.** See on *cares*, I, i, 16.

In this scene, note the Masque in rhyme, lines 60-138. Such pieces, with dancing, singing, splendid scenery, exquisite music, and with highborn gentlemen and ladies for actors, were very fashionable in the reigns of Elizabeth, James, and the first Charles. Some have supposed that this was intended for presentation at the marriage of the Earl of Essex and Lady Frances Howard in 1611.

"Darwin claims for the bonnet-monkey 'the forehead which gives to man his noble and intellectual appearance'; and it is obvious that it was not wanting in Caliban, for when he discovers the true quality of the drunken fools he has mistaken for gods, his remonstrance is, 'we shall all be turned to apes with foreheads villanous low.' . . . Caliban is not a brutalized, but a natural brute mind. He is a being in whom the moral instincts of man have no part; but also in whom the degradation of savage humanity is equally wanting. He is a novel anthropoid of a high type, — such as on the hypothesis of evolution must have existed intermediately between the ape and man, — in whom some spark of rational intelligence has been enkindled, under the tutorship of one who has already mastered the secrets of nature. . . . Caliban seems indeed the half-human link between the brute and man." — Dr. Daniel Wilson's *Caliban: the Missing Link*, 1873.

ACT V.

Scene I. *Before the Cell of Prospero.*

Enter Prospero *in his magic robes, and* Ariel.

Prospero. Now does my project gather to a head;
My charms crack not, my spirits obey, and Time
Goes upright with his carriage. How's the day?
 Ariel. On the sixth hour; at which time, my lord,
You said our work should cease.
 Prospero.   I did say so,
When first I rais'd the tempest. Say, my spirit,
How fares the king and's followers?
 Ariel.   Confin'd together
In the same fashion as you gave in charge,
Just as you left them; all prisoners, sir,
In the line-grove which weather-fends your cell: 10
They cannot budge till your release. The king,
His brother, and yours, abide all three distracted,
And the remainder mourning over them,
Brimful of sorrow and dismay; but chiefly

Act V. Scene I. **1. my project,** etc. "Prospero's departure from the island is the abandoning by Shakespeare of the theatre, the scene of his marvellous works: 'Graves at my command Have waked their sleepers, oped, and let them forth By my so potent art.' Henceforth Prospero is but a man; no longer a great enchanter. He returns to the dukedom he had lost in Stratford-upon-Avon, and will pay no tribute henceforth to any Alonzo or Lucy of them all." *Dowden.*—2. **crack not** = are without a flaw [Wright]? break not (as magic bands) [Allen]?—3. **carriage** = chariot? load (under which, Time, as an old man, bends) [Warburton]?—In *Hamlet,* V, ii, 149, 'carriages' are sword-straps; in *Acts,* xxi, 15, luggage; in *Merry Wives of W.*, II, ii, 155, it is that which is carried (a bag of money).—9. To make this line metrical, Abbott, 484, would divide '*all*' into two syllables (á-ll), and squeeze 'prisoners' into 'pris'ners'! Reed would transpose *sir* to follow *them.*—10. **line-grove.** IV, i, 193.—**weather-fends.** *Fend* = to ward off. Shortened from obs. *fendere,* to strike. *Skeat.*—11. **budge.** Fr. *bouger,* to stir; fr. Lat. *bullicare,* frequentative of *bulbire,* to boil; Ital. *bulicare,* to bubble up.

Him that you term'd, sir, the good old lord, Gonzalo:
His tears run down his beard, like winter's drops
From eaves of reeds. Your charm so strongly works 'em
That if you now beheld them, your affections
Would become tender.
   Prospero. Dost thou think so, spirit?
   Ariel. Mine would, sir, were I human.
   Prospero. And mine shall.
Hast thou, which art but air, a touch, a feeling   21
Of their afflictions, and shall not myself,
One of their kind, that relish all as sharply
Passion as they, be kindlier mov'd than thou art?
Though with their high wrongs I am struck to the quick,
Yet with my nobler reason 'gainst my fury
Do I take part. The rarer action is
In virtue than in vengeance; they being penitent,
The sole drift of my purpose doth extend
Not a frown further. Go release them, Ariel;   30
My charms I'll break, their senses I'll restore,
And they shall be themselves.
   Ariel. I'll fetch them, sir. [*Exit.*
   Prospero. Ye elves of hills, brooks, standing lakes, and
      groves,
And ye that on the sands with printless foot
Do chase the ebbing Neptune, and do fly him   35
When he comes back; you demi-puppets that
By moonshine do the green sour ringlets make,

Brachet.—15. **him** = he [Furness]?—*Him* is often put for 'he' by 'attraction.' *Abbott,* 208. Here, according to Abbott, the relative to which 'him' is attracted, is *that.*—May we supply, mentally, 'I refer especially to,' before *him?*—23. **relish all as sharply, Passion as they** = relish all passion as sharply as they do? or relish passion all (i.e. full) as sharply as they do [Holt, Walker, Furness]? feel as keenly the emotions of joy and express sorrow as they do [Wright, who retains the comma of folios 1, 2, after 'sharply,' and makes 'passion' a verb]? **Passion** = feel the force of passion [Theobald]? express emotion [Schmidt]? —24–30. This very significant Christian spirit breathes through all the plays of Shakespeare's latest period.—33–50. **Ye elves,** etc. Here are traces of Shakespeare's acquaintance both with the original of Medea's incantation in Ovid's *Metamorphoses* (vii, 197-219) and with Golding's translation of the same in 1567. "Ovid," says Maginn (*Fraser's Magazine,* October, 1839), "has contributed to the invocation of Prospero at least as much as Golding."—Evidently the story of Medea had deeply impressed Shakespeare's imagination. 2 *Henry IV,* V, ii, 59; *Mer. of Ven.,* V, i, 13.—34. **printless foot.** *Comus,* 897.—35. **Neptune.** I, ii, 433.—36. **demi-puppets.** Why *demi?*—37. **green sour ringlets** =

Whereof the ewe not bites; and you whose pastime
Is to make midnight mushrooms, that rejoice
To hear the solemn curfew; by whose aid— 40
Weak masters though ye be — I have bedimm'd
The noontide sun, call'd forth the mutinous winds,
And 'twixt the green sea and the azur'd vault
Set roaring war: to the dread rattling thunder
Have I given fire, and rifted Jove's stout oak
With his own bolt; the strong-bas'd promontory
Have I made shake, and by the spurs pluck'd up
The pine and cedar; graves at my command
Have wak'd their sleepers, op'd, and let 'em forth
By my so potent art. But this rough magic 50
I here abjure; and, when I have requir'd
Some heavenly music — which even now I do, —
To work mine end upon their senses that
This airy charm is for, I'll break my staff,
Bury it certain fathoms in the earth,
And deeper than did ever plummet sound
I'll drown my book. [*Solemn music.*

Here enter ARIEL *before: then* ALONSO, *with a frantic gesture, attended by* GONZALO; SEBASTIAN *and* ANTONIO *in like manner, attended by* ADRIAN *and* FRANCISCO: *they all enter the circle which* PROSPERO *had made, and there stand charmed; which* PROSPERO *observing, speaks:*

A solemn air, and the best comforter
To an unsettled fancy, cure thy brains,
Now useless, boil'd within thy skull! There stand, 60
For you are spell-stopp'd. —
Holy Gonzalo, honorable man,

'fairy rings'? Grey (*Crit., Hist., and Explan. Notes*, 1754) says that these little rings 'are higher, sourer, and of a deeper green than the grass which grows around them.' They are 'the circles formed in grassy lawns by certain fungi (as *Marasmius Oreades*), formerly supposed to be caused by fairies in their midnight dances.' Webster's *Int. Dict.* — 38. **not bites.** 113; II, i, 118. — 39, 40. **rejoice to hear the solemn curfew.** Our *Comus*, 432–435. — 41. **weak masters** = inferior masters of these supernatural powers [Steevens]? powerful auxiliaries, but weak if left to yourselves [Blackstone]? weak proficients, weak adepts [Furness]? — In 'masters' Jephson discovers slightly contemptuous irony; Rolfe, affectionate irony. — 43. **azur'd.** Adjective turned to verb? *Abbott*, 294. — 45, 46. **Jove's**, etc. Oak and thunderbolt, sacred to Jove? *As You Like It*, III, ii, 221. — 53. **that** = which? whom?
  60. **boil'd.** There is in this word an energy amounting to fierceness.

Mine eyes, even sociable to the show of thine,
Fall fellowly drops. — The charm dissolves apace;
And as the morning steals upon the night,
Melting the darkness, so their rising senses
Begin to chase the ignorant fumes that mantle
Their clearer reason. — O good Gonzalo,
My true preserver, and a royal sir
To him thou follow'st! I will pay thy graces   70
Home both in word and deed. — Most cruelly
Didst thou, Alonso, use me and my daughter;
Thy brother was a furtherer in the act. —
Thou art pinch'd for't now, Sebastian. — Flesh and blood,
You, brother mine, that entertain'd ambition,
Expell'd remorse and nature; who, with Sebastian, —
Whose inward pinches therefore are most strong, —
Would here have kill'd your king; I do forgive thee,
Unnatural though thou art. — Their understanding
Begins to swell, and the approaching tide   80
Will shortly fill the reasonable shore
That now lies foul and muddy. Not one of them
That yet looks on me, or would know me. — Ariel,
Fetch me the hat and rapier in my cell;
I will discase me, and myself present
As I was sometime Milan. Quickly, spirit;
Thou shalt ere long be free.

See *Wint. Tale*, III, iii, 63; 'seething brains' in *Mid. N. Dr.*, V, i, 4. — 63. **sociable to the show** = sympathizing with what appears [Rolfe]? in close companionship and sympathy with the appearance [Wright]? — 64. **fall.** II, i, 292; *As Y. L. I.*, III, v, 5. — **fellowly.** III, i, 84; our *Jul. Cæs.*, III, i, 62. — The *-ly*, in *fellowly*, is A. S. *lic*, like. — Abbott, 447. — 67. **ignorant** = of ignorance [Wright]? causing ignorance [Furness]? — *Fumes* personified? — **mantle.** IV, i, 182. — 71. **home** = completely? — Shakes. uses 'home' = 'to the quick,' or 'sensibly,' 'effectively,' 'earnestly.' — 75. **You.** III, iii, 56. — 76. **remorse** = pity? tender affection? compunction of conscience? — Lat. *re*, again; *mordēre*, to bite; *remorsus*, biting back, biting again and again. Our *Macb.*, I, v, 42; *Mer. of Ven.*, IV, i, 20. — 77. **thee.** *Thou*, from a superior to an inferior, is often confidential, good-humored. "But a master, finding fault, often resorts to the unfamiliar 'you,' much as Cæsar cut his soldiers to the heart by giving them the respectful title of 'Quirites.'" — 81. **reasonable** = of reason? rational, appropriate, conformable to reason? — "The shore of reason which has just been, by another figure, compared to clear water covered with a scum of ignorant fumes." *Wright.* — See on *ignorant*, line 67. — 85. **discase.** In *Wint. T.*, IV, iii, 616-618, we have, "make an exchange; therefore discase thee instantly . . . change garments," etc. — In *Meas. for M.*, II, iv, we read 'thy case, thy habit.' — 86. **sometime.** So 'our sometime sister,' *Hamlet*, I, ii, 8; *Ephes.*, ii, 13.

ARIEL *sings, and helps to attire him.*

> *Where the bee sucks, there suck I:*
> *In a cowslip's bell I lie;*
> *There I couch when owls do cry.* 90
> *On the bat's back I do fly*
> *After summer merrily.*
> *Merrily, merrily, shall I live now*
> *Under the blossom that hangs on the bough.*

Prospero. Why, that's my dainty Ariel! I shall miss thee;
But yet thou shalt have freedom: — so, so, so. —
To the king's ship, invisible as thou art:
There shalt thou find the mariners asleep
Under the hatches; the master and the boatswain
Being awake, enforce them to this place, 100
And presently, I prithee.
 Ariel. I drink the air before me, and return
Or ere your pulse twice beat. [*Exit.*
 Gonzalo. All torment, trouble, wonder, and amazement
Inhabits here; some heavenly power guide us
Out of this fearful country!
 Prospero. Behold, sir king,
The wronged Duke of Milan, Prospero!

88-94. We leave to the botanists and ornithologists their disputes over this pretty song. Those who are curious about them may read the quotations and references in *Furness*, and we wish them much joy of the owl and the bat. "What," says Furness, "has natural history to do with *The Tempest*, where all is unnatural history? as if a spirit, that could tread the ooze of the salt deep or work i' the veins of the earth when it is bak'd with frost, could not fly, if it chose, in perpetual sunshine, on the back of a bat, which was torpid as a stone with the cold of a dozen winters." — 96. **so, so, so.** Referring to Ariel's assistance in attiring him [Furness]? —100. **being awake.** "Nom. absolute," says *Abbott*, 376; but —? — 101. **presently.** I, ii, 125; IV, i, 42. —102. **drink the air.** "It would be difficult to parallel this little speech," say the Cowden-Clarkes (in their *The Plays of Shakespeare*, London ed.), "with one conveying an equal impression of swift motion. Shakespeare himself has matched it in his Puck's 'I'll put a girdle round about the earth in forty minutes,' and, 'I go, I go, look how I go; swifter than arrow from the Tartar's bow'; where the words seem to dart out with the speed and light leaps of Robin Goodfellow himself." — *Drink the air* is like 'devour the way,' *2 Henry IV*, I, i, 47; *viam vorabit*, will swallow the way, Catullus, xxxv, 7.— **or ere.** Note on I, ii, 11. — 105. **inhabits.** This form in *s*, where we should expect the 'singular,' is very common in *S.* Abbott, 333, 336, thinks *s* was still

For more assurance that a living prince
Does now speak to thee, I embrace thy body;
And to thee and thy company I bid   110
A hearty welcome.
   Alonso.   Whether thou beest he or no,
Or some enchanted trifle to abuse me,
As late I have been, I not know: thy pulse
Beats, as of flesh and blood; and, since I saw thee,
The affliction of my mind amends, with which,
I fear, a madness held me. This must crave —
And if this be at all — a most strange story.
Thy dukedom I resign, and do entreat
Thou pardon me my wrongs. — But how should Prospero
Be living and be here?
   Prospero.   First, noble friend,   120
Let me embrace thine age, whose honor cannot
Be measur'd or confined.
   Gonzalo.   Whether this be
Or be not, I'll not swear.
   Prospero.   You do yet taste
Some subtleties o' the isle, that will not let you
Believe things certain. — Welcome, my friends all! —
[*Aside to Sebastian and Antonio*] But you, my brace of
       lords, were I so minded,
I here could pluck his highness' frown upon you,
And justify you traitors; at this time
I'll tell no tales.

---

recognized as a relic of the E. Eng. plu. in *s* or *es*. — 112. **enchanted trifle** = bewitching phantom [Hudson]? trifle produced by enchantment [Walker]? — The old sense of *trifle* was a delusion, a trick. *Skeat.* — **abuse** = deceive. *Hamlet*, II, ii, 590, and often in *S*. — 113. **not know.** 38, 304; II, i, 118. — **saw.** Abbott, 347. — 117. **And if.** So the folio. Icel. *enda*, if. See our *Jul. Cæs.*, I, ii, 257; *Matt.*, xxiv, 48, 'But and if that evil servant,' etc. Abbott, 101–105. — 119. **wrongs** = sins? Line 25. — 123. **subtleties.** A 'subtlety' denoted a device in pastry and confectionery. Says Steevens, "When a dish was so contrived as to appear unlike what it really was, they called it a *subtilty*. Dragons, castles, trees, etc., made out of sugar had the like denomination. Froissart complains much of this practice, which often led him into mistakes at dinner." "I am afraid Steevens is right." *Furness.* — 127. **pluck.** A. S. *pluccian*, to pull. The butcher's term ('pluck') arose from *pulling* the vital organs from the slain animal. *Skeat.* — 128. **justify** = exculpate? prove just? prove? — In *All's W. T. E. W.*, IV, iii, 50, 51, *justified* = proved. — 129. **No!** Hudson, Meiklejohn, and some others follow Allen (*Phila. Shake. Soc.*) and read *Now* instead of 'No'; because, they say,

SCENE I.] *THE TEMPEST.* 121

Sebastian [*Aside*] The devil speaks in him.
Prospero.   NO! —
For you, most wicked sir, whom to call brother   130
Would even infect my mouth, I do forgive
Thy rankest fault, — all of them; and require
My dukedom of thee, which perforce I know
Thou must restore.
  Alonso.   If thou beest Prospero,
Give us particulars of thy preservation;
How thou hast met us here, who three hours since
Were wrack'd upon this shore, where I have lost —
How sharp the point of this remembrance is! —
My dear son Ferdinand.
  Prospero.   I am woe for't, sir.
  Alonso. Irreparable is the loss, and patience   140
Says it is past her cure.
  Prospero.   I rather think
You have not sought her help, of whose soft grace
For the like loss I have her sovereign aid,
And rest myself content.
  Alonso.   You the like loss?
  Prospero. As great to me as late; and supportable
To make the dear loss have I means much weaker
Than you may call to comfort you, for I
Have lost my daughter.

Prospero could not have heard Sebastian's remark. But magicians have good ears. Prospero's indignant *No* is as forcible as *Now* would be tame. — 132. **rankest** = of highest grade? most malodorous? — Fr. *rang*, range, rank; A. S. *ranc*, strong, proud, forward. The sense of 'strong-scented' is late, due to confusion with Lat. *rancidus*, rancid, or rather with O. Fr. *rance*, 'musty, fusty, stale.' *Skeat.* — 136. **who.** The 1st folio has *whom*, which, possibly, from the proximity of *us*, might be explained as a case of 'attraction.' — 139. **woe** = sorry [Malone, Hudson, Phillpotts, Rolfe, Meiklejohn]? — *Abbott*, 230, calls the sentence 'an ungrammatical remnant of an ancient usage,' for "Woe is [to] me." May it be that Prospero means "I am woe itself, an embodiment of woe"? See 'blasphemy,' line 218; 'conduct,' 244; 'cramp,' 287. — 145. **as late** = and has as lately happened [Johnson, Hudson, Meiklejohn, Deighton]? as it is recent [Wright, Rolfe]? — The folio has a comma after 'me.' Which interpretation does the comma favor? — **supportable.** How accented? Abbott divides thus:

As gréat | to mé | as láte; | *and* suppórt | ablé.

This seems to make a bull of the last syllable. Perhaps it would be better to accent the 1st and 3d syl. of 'supportable.' — 146. **dear.** II, i, 132. — 148. **daughter.** Walker and Dyce tell us *daughter* is a trisyllable! They do not tell us how. We may therefore guess. Try *daugh—a—ter!* or

Alonso.   A daughter?
O heavens, that they were living both in Naples,
The king and queen there! that they were, I wish   150
Myself were mudded in that oozy bed
Where my son lies. When did you lose your daughter?
  Prospero. In this last tempest. I perceive, these lords
At this encounter do so much admire
That they devour their reason, and scarce think
Their eyes do offices of truth, their words
Are natural breath: but, howsoe'er you have
Been justled from your senses, know for certain
That I am Prospero, and that very duke
Which was thrust forth of Milan; who most strangely   160
Upon this shore, where you were wrack'd, was landed,
To be the lord on't. No more yet of this;
For 'tis a chronicle of day by day,
Not a relation for a breakfast, nor
Befitting this first meeting. Welcome, sir;
This cell's my court: here have I few attendants,
And subjects none abroad; pray you, look in.
My dukedom since you have given me again,
I will requite you with as good a thing;
At least bring forth a wonder, to content ye   170
As much as me my dukedom.

Here PROSPERO *discovers* FERDINAND *and* MIRANDA *playing at chess.*

  Miranda. Sweet lord, you play me false.

---

daugh—augh—ter! or, possibly, *daugh—ter—er!* Any one of these would be dreadful, if it were not so irresistibly funny. Fill out the metre by a long pause, such as the sense naturally requires. See our *Hamlet*, I, i, 129, 132, 135.— 150. **that** = provided that?— 154. **admire**. Lat. *ad, at; mirari,* to wonder.— See *admired, Par. Lost*, ii, 677.— 155. **devour**. III, iii, 84.— 156. **their words** = even their own words? But Capell and Hudson change *their* to 'these.' Wisely?— 160. **which ... of.** *Abbott*, 266, 166.— 170. **content ye** = please you? Fr. *contenter*, to satisfy, gratify. As for *ye*, it is often used similarly in *Shakes.* and by Milton, Bayard Taylor, etc. *Abbott*, 236.

  172. **discovers** = discloses? finds?— Fr. *découvrir,* to uncover, bring to view. The etymology is curious. Lat. *dis,* apart; O. Fr. *des,* Fr. *de;* Lat. *co-* or *con-*, together, with, completely; *ob,* towards, against, over; root PER or PAR, to complete, make (or cover?); Lat. *operire,* to conceal; *cooperire,* to cover over, or cover entirely; whence *couvrir,* to cover; and *découvrir.*— **chess**. In the Elizabethan age, Naples is said to have been the headquarters of this game.— **play me.** *Abbott*, 220.

Ferdinand. No, my dear'st love,
I would not for the world.
  Miranda. Yes, for a score of kingdoms you should wrangle,
And I would call it fair play.
  Alonso. If this prove
A vision of the island, one dear son
Shall I twice lose.
  Sebastian. A most high miracle!
  Ferdinand. Though the seas threaten, they are merciful;
I have curs'd them without cause. [*Kneels.*
  Alonso. Now all the blessings
Of a glad father compass thee about! 180
Arise, and say how thou cam'st here.
  Miranda. O, wonder!
How many goodly creatures are there here!
How beauteous mankind is! O brave new world
That has such people in't!
  Prospero. 'Tis new to thee.
  Alonso. What is this maid with whom thou wast at play?
Your eld'st acquaintance cannot be three hours;
Is she the goddess that hath sever'd us,
And brought us thus together?
  Ferdinand. Sir, she is mortal,
But by immortal Providence she's mine;
I chose her when I could not ask my father 190
For his advice, nor thought I had one. She
Is daughter to this famous Duke of Milan
Of whom so often I have heard renown,
But never saw before; of whom I have
Receiv'd a second life, and second father
This lady makes him to me.

---

175. **score** = (not the number twenty but) account (subject or bet) [Warburton]? twenty [Johnson]? *Score of kingdoms* = game in which the score is reckoned by kingdoms [Wright]? stake? wager? — **wrangle** = dispute noisily? wrong me [Hudson]? — A. S. *wringan*, to press; past, *wrang*, pressed. M. Eng. *wranglen*. . . . The frequentative of *wring*, to press, to strain. . . . The orig. sense was to keep on pressing, to urge; hence to argue vehemently. *Skeat.* — Does she mean, "If kingdoms were at stake, and you disputed my charge of cheating, (I am in such a state of mind that) I should call it fair play"? — 176. **vision of the island.** In Act III, sc. iii, he has seen one or two visions vanish into nothingness. — 182, 183. **goodly . . . beauteous,** etc. *Goodly*, as in *Hamlet*, I, ii, 186, is good-looking? So Milton's 'Adam, the goodliest man,' *Par. Lost,* iv, 323. It must be remembered that they were dressed in fine apparel, I, ii, 218, 219. — 187. **Is she the goddess.** *Æneid,* i, 328, 329; *Comus,*

Alonso. I am hers.
But, O, how oddly will it sound that I
Must ask my child forgiveness!
　Prospero. There, sir, stop;
Let us not burthen our remembrances with
A heaviness that's gone.
　Gonzalo. I have inly wept, 200
Or should have spoke ere this. — Look down, you gods,
And on this couple drop a blessed crown!
For it is you that have chalk'd forth the way
Which brought us hither.
　Alonso. I say Amen, Gonzalo!
　Gonzalo. Was Milan thrust from Milan, that his issue 205
Should become kings of Naples? O, rejoice
Beyond a common joy! and set it down
With gold on lasting pillars: In one voyage
Did Claribel her husband find at Tunis;
And Ferdinand her brother found a wife, 210
Where he himself was lost; Prospero his dukedom,
In a poor isle; and all of us ourselves,
When no man was his own.
　Alonso. [*to Ferdinand and Miranda*] Give me your hands;
Let grief and sorrow still embrace his heart
That doth not wish you joy!
　Gonzalo. Be it so! Amen! —

Enter ARIEL, *with the* Master *and* Boatswain *amazedly following.*

O, look, sir! look, sir! here is more of us!
I prophesied, if a gallows were on land,

266, 267. — 196. **hers** = her second father? — 199. **remembrances.** Allen, Furness, and some others would not sound the *s*, and Furness would elide it and put an apostrophe to indicate the elision. Would not such apostrophe, however, convey to the average reader an erroneous notion; viz., that the word is in the possessive case? — "It is sufficient for a word to terminate in the sound of *s* to be regarded by the ear as a plural." *Furness* (referring to *Walker*, Vers. 246; *Abbott*, 471). See on 'princess,' I, ii, 173. — 200. **heaviness.** *Mer. of V.*, V, i, 130; *Jul. Cæs.*, II, i, 275. — 203. **chalk'd forth the way.** So in *Henry VIII*, I, i, 60, 'chalks successors their way.' — 213. **his own** = in his senses [Steevens, Hudson]? master of himself [Rolfe, Deighton]? — Is the phrase 'self-possessed' quite equivalent? — Considering lines 205–213, Phillpotts thinks the play might well have been called, "Lost but Found." — 214. **still** = up to this time? always? continually? — I, ii, 229; III, iii, 64.

This fellow could not drown. — Now, blasphemy,
That swear'st grace o'erboard, not an oath on shore?
Hast thou no mouth by land? What is the news? 220
    Boatswain. The best news is, that we have safely found
Our king and company; the next, our ship —
Which, but three glasses since, we gave out split —

---

216. **here is.** I, i, 16; ii, 477. — 221. **safely found** = found safe. Rolfe remarks, "Shakespeare often uses adverbs as 'predicate adjectives,' a fact not mentioned by Abbott." Rolfe cites 'look wearily,' III, i, 32; 'looks successfully' in *As You L. I.*, I, ii, 137, etc. — 223. **three glasses,** etc. This sentence and that uttered by Helena in *All's Well* (II, i, 165, 166) are relied upon as 'a sure proof that Shakespeare *never was at sea.*' The elaborate argument to this effect by Br. Nicholson (*New Shakespeare Soc. Trans.*, 1880–2, P't i, p. 53) is quoted with approbation by Furness (*Var. Ed., The Tempest*, pp. 255, 256). Briefly, he urges that the seaman's 'glass' is always a half-hour glass; that Prospero or Ariel (I, ii, 239–241), just after the storm had ceased, said it was 'at least two glasses,' meaning *hours,* past midday; that Alonzo had specified less than *three hours* (V, i, 186) as the time that had elapsed since Ferdinand made the acquaintance of Miranda; that the boatswain's 'three glasses' in this line must therefore cover three hours; that the 'four and twenty times the pilot's glass,' spoken of by Helena in *All's Well,* cannot mark half-hours; and therefore, to conclude, we must abandon the long-cherished belief in Shakespeare's accuracy in the technology of navigation. In reply, it may be suggested that a *landman* would naturally understand the word glass as meaning 'the sandy hour-glass' of *Mer. of Ven.*, I, i, 25; that in *All's Well,* Helena is not a sailor, nor bound to be technically accurate, and she very likely speaks of twenty-four *hours,*[1] though she uses the words, 'four and twenty times the pilot's glass'; that the expression 'at least two glasses' (*Tempest,* I, ii, 240) is neither spoken by nor to a sailor, but by Prospero to Ariel, both accustomed to *hour-glasses;* that the remark, "it cannot be three hours" proves nothing as to the mode of reckoning. It was past two when the lovers first met. The boatswain is not a good witness as to the lapse of time; (*a*) having probably taken too many glasses of a different sort (I, i, 50); (*b*) having been sound asleep (I, ii, 32; V, i, 230, 231); and (*c*) being disposed to heighten the miracle by shortening the time (V, i, 223). Wherefore, may we not still have faith in Shakespeare's technical knowledge of seamanship? — **gave out** = gave

---

[1] The king asks her how soon her mysterious medicine can cure his malady. She answers virtually in a *climax,* first, less than two days; secondly, about a day and a half; thirdly, less than one day; thus:

    "Ere twice the horses of the sun shall bring
      Their fiery torcher his diurnal ring;   [i.e. two full days.]
      Ere twice in murk and occidental damp
      Moist Hesperus hath quenched his sleepy lamp;   [say 36 hours?]
      Or four and twenty times the pilot's glass
      Hath told the thievish minutes how they pass."   [twenty-four hours.]

If this interpretation of the passage in *All's Well* is not correct, are we not forced to the conclusion that Helena simply repeats herself in utter tautology, 'ere two days, ere two days, ere two days'? Mr. P. A. Daniel in his *Time Analysis,* tells us "the pilot's glass in *All's Well* is a two-hour glass"! Furness concurs in this. Was then the king so stupid as to require such — iteration?

Is tight, and yare, and bravely rigg'd as when
We first put out to sea.
 Ariel. [*Aside to Prospero*] Sir, all this service
Have I done since I went.
 Prospero. [*Aside to Ariel*] My tricksy spirit!
 Alonso. These are not natural events; they strengthen
From strange to stranger.—Say, how came you hither?
 Boatswain. If I did think, sir, I were well awake,
I'd strive to tell you. We were dead of sleep,   230
And—how we know not—all clapp'd under hatches;
Where, but even now, with strange and several noises
Of roaring, shrieking, howling, jingling chains,
And moe diversity of sounds, all horrible,
We were awak'd; straightway, at liberty;
Where we, in all her trim, freshly beheld
Our royal, good, and gallant ship; our master
Capering to eye her. On a trice, so please you,
Even in a dream, were we divided from them
And were brought moping hither.
 Ariel. [*Aside to Prospero*]   Was't well done?   240
 Prospero. [*Aside to Ariel*] Bravely, my diligence. Thou
   shalt be free.
 Alonso. This is as strange a maze as e'er men trod;
And there is in this business more than nature
Was ever conduct of: some oracle
Must rectify our knowledge.
 Prospero.   Sir, my liege,
Do not infest your mind with beating on
The strangeness of this business. At pick'd leisure,
Which shall be shortly, single I'll resolve you,
Which to you shall seem probable, of every

---

up as [Rolfe]? believed and declared to be [Deighton]?—224. **yare.** I, i, 3.—226. **tricksy.** Du. *treckken*, to draw; *trek*, a trick. Our *Mer. of Ven.*, III, v, 50; *Hamlet*, IV, vii, 186.—230. **of sleep.** *Abbott*, 168.—232. **several.** III, i, 42.—240. **moping.** IV, i, 47: our *Hamlet*, III, iv, 81.—244. **conduct** = conductor? So said to be in *Richard II*, IV, i, 157; *Rom. and Jul.*, V, iii, 116. See 'blasphemy,' line 218; 'diligence.' 241, etc.—246. **infest.** Lat. *in*, against; obs. *fedère* or *jendère*, to strike; *infestare*, to attack.—**beating on.** I, ii, 176; *Hamlet*, III, i, 174.—248. **single** = by myself [Wright]? single, one by one [Delius]? in private [Rolfe, Deighton, Meiklejohn]? to you (Alonso) alone [Warburton, Capell, Furness]—**resolve.** Our *Jul. Cæs.*, III, i, 132. Do we say 'solve doubts'?—249. **which.** What? solution? explanation [Allen]? method [Johnson]?—**probable** = deserving approbation [Johnson]? proved

These happen'd accidents; till when, be cheerful, 256
And think of each thing well. — [*Aside to Ariel*] Come hither,
    spirit:
Set Caliban and his companions free;
Untie the spell. — [*Exit Ariel*] How fares my gracious sir?
There are yet missing of your company
Some few odd lads that you remember not.

Enter ARIEL, *driving in* CALIBAN, STEPHANO, *and* TRINCULO,
     in their stolen apparel.

Stephano. Every man shift for all the rest, and let no man take care for himself, for all is but fortune. — Coragio, bully-monster, coragio!

Trinculo. If these be true spies which I wear in my head, here's a goodly sight. 260

Caliban. O Setebos, these be brave spirits indeed!
How fine my master is! I am afraid
He will chastise me.

Sebastian.   Ha, ha!
What things are these, my lord Antonio?
Will money buy 'em?

Antonio.   Very like; one of them
Is a plain fish, and no doubt marketable.

Prospero. Mark but the badges of these men, my lords,
Then say if they be true. — This misshapen knave,
His mother was a witch; and one so strong
That could control the moon, make flows and ebbs, 270
And deal in her command without her power.

[Allen]? — "It seems to me quite sufficient that Prospero's resolution [explanation?] should appear 'probable' to Alonso, especially if we take 'seem' in its strongest sense." *Furness.* Abbott, 271. — **every.** *Abbott,* 12. — 250. **happen'd.** *Abbott,* 295. — 253. **untie.** See III, iii, 89; I, ii, 485. — 255. **odd** = unnoticed? queer? — Icel. *oddi*, a triangle; a point of land; Dan. *od*, a point. 'Odds and ends' = points and ends. The sense of 'strange' or 'queer' seems to be a mere development from that of uneven. *Skeat.*
    259. **Coragio** [Ital.] = courage. Lat. *cor*, heart; Fr. *courage.* — 261. **Setebos.** I, ii, 371. — 267. **badges** = stolen apparel? — "Household servants usually wore on their arms, as a part of their livery, silver 'badges,' whereon the shield of their masters was engraved." *Furness.* — 268. **if they** = if the badges [Furness]? if the men [Johnson]? — **true** = genuine [Furness]? honest [Johnson]? — 271. **without** = beyond [Staunton, Wright, Hudson, Furness, Meiklejohn]? — **without her power,** etc. = exercise her rule without being empowered by her to do so, usurping her authority [Malone, Dyce, Rolfe, Phillpotts, Deighton]? **exercise,**

These three have robb'd me; and this demi-devil —
For he's a bastard one — had plotted with them
To take my life. Two of these fellows you
Must know and own; this thing of darkness I
Acknowledge mine.
  Caliban.   I shall be pinch'd to death.
  Alonso. Is not this Stephano, my drunken butler?
  Sebastian. He is drunk now; where had he wine?
  Alonso. And Trinculo is reeling-ripe; where should they
Find this grand liquor that hath gilded 'em?   280
How cam'st thou in this pickle?
  Trinculo. I have been in such a pickle, since I saw you
last, that, I fear me, will never out of my bones; I shall not
fear fly-blowing.
  Sebastian. Why, how now, Stephano!
  Stephano. O, touch me not; I am not Stephano, but a
cramp.
  Prospero. You'd be king o' the isle, sirrah?
  Stephano. I should have been a sore one, then.
  Alonso. This is a strange thing as e'er I look'd on.   290
                            [*Pointing to Caliban.*
  Prospero. He is as disproportion'd in his manners
As in his shape. — Go, sirrah, to my cell;
Take with you your companions; as you look
To have my pardon, trim it handsomely.
  Caliban. Ay, that I will; and I'll be wise hereafter,
And seek for grace. What a thrice-double ass
Was I, to take this drunkard for a god,
And worship this dull fool!

---

locally and exceptionally, the office of the moon, but *without her power* as a universal cause of the tidal action [Knight]? *beyond* her power [Staunton, Furness]? outdo the moon in exercising the moon's own command [Hudson]? In *2 Corinth.*, x, 13, 'without our measure' = beyond our measure. — 279. **reeling ripe** = ripe for reeling [Wright, Rolfe]? So drunk that he reels [Deighton]? — In *Love's L. L.*, V, ii, 275, and in Sidney's *Arcadia* (1598), p. 61, we have 'weeping ripe'; in *Com. of Er.*, I, i, 77, 'sinking ripe'; *Beaum. and Fletch.*, 'crying ripe,' and 'drunk and tumbling ripe.' — 280. **gilded.** Anciently used for intoxicated, Theobald, Warburton, Steevens, Wright, etc., see an allusion to the *Elixor* of the alchemists (*aurum potabile*, Milton's 'potable gold.' *Par. Lost*, iii, 608). In 'gilded,' Phillpotts sees a double play: (1) on their clothes; (2) on sack (sherry) as the true elixir. — 283. **fear me** = permit myself to fear? fear for myself? *Abbott*, 296. — 289. **sore.** Some find a quibble here, and similarly in *2 Henry VI*, IV, vii, 9. — 290. Ellipsis? *Abbott*, 276. — 296. **grace.** Everyone is forgiven, and even Caliban will begin a

Prospero. Go to; away!
Alonso. Hence, and bestow your luggage where you found it.
Sebastian. Or stole it, rather.   300
          [*Exeunt Caliban, Stephano, and Trinculo.*
Prospero. Sir, I invite your highness and your train
To my poor cell, where you shall take your rest
For this one night; which, part of it, I'll waste
With such discourse as, I not doubt, shall make it
Go quick away,—the story of my life,
And the particular accidents gone by
Since I came to this isle: and in the morn
I'll bring you to your ship, and so to Naples,
Where I have hope to see the nuptial
Of these our dear-belov'd solemnized;   310
And thence retire me to my Milan, where
Every third thought shall be my grave.
      Alonso.   I long
To hear the story of your life, which must
Take the ear strangely.
      Prospero.   I'll deliver all;
And promise you calm seas, auspicious gales,
And sail so expeditious that shall catch
Your royal fleet far off.—[*Aside to Ariel*] My Ariel, chick,
That is thy charge; then to the elements
Be free, and fare thou well!—Please you, draw near.
                                           [*Exeunt.*

---

better life!—299. **bestow.** *2 Kings,* v, 24.—304, II, i, 118; *Abbott,* 305.
—309. **nuptial.** S. prefers the 'singular' form of this word, but uses the plural also.—310. **solemnized.** Shakes. here, and Milton in *Par. Lost,* vii, 448, accent the 2d syl.—311. **retire me.** *Abbott,* 296.—314. **deliver.** II, i, 45.—317. **fleet far off.** I, ii, 234.—319. **please you** = may it please you? if it please you?

"Stephano and Trinculo sum up the old distrust of the lower classes. They are not a mob, to be sure; on the magic island there was no chance for a mob to breed; in Stephano and Trinculo, however, all the folly and the impotence of a mob are incarnate. With Caliban the case is different; in him there is a perception of something not hinted at before.

"The single unique figure of Caliban, in short, typifies the whole history of such world-wide social evolution, such permanent race-conflict, as was only beginning in Shakespeare's day, and is not ended in our own. Civilization, exploring and advancing, comes face to face with barbarism and savagery. Savage and barbarian alike absorb, not the blessings of civilization, but its vices, amid which their own simple virtues are lost. Ruin follows. . . . Humanity forbids the massacre of the lower races; the equally noble instinct of race-supremacy forbids any but a suicidally

EPILOGUE.

SPOKEN BY PROSPERO.

Now my charms are all o'erthrown,
And what strength I have's mine own,
Which is most faint; now, 'tis true,
I must be here confin'd by you,
Or sent to Naples. Let me not,
Since I have my dukedom got,
And pardon'd the deceiver, dwell
In this bare island by your spell;
But release me from my bands

---

philanthropic man of European blood to contemplate without almost equal horror the thought of miscegenation. Where Caliban would possess Miranda, we torment Caliban, but still we feel bound to preserve him,— which [sic] is not good for the morals or the temper of Caliban. That savage figure, then, shows a vision so prophetic that at least one modern scholar has chosen to study in Caliban the psychology of Darwin's missing link. Marvellously prophetic suggestiveness, however, is not exactly a condition of theatrical effect." — Wendell's *William Shakespeare*, 1894.

EPILOGUE. Prologues and epilogues, it is said, were often written in the Elizabethan age by other persons than the authors of the plays. Richard Grant White and some others are quite sure that such was the case with this. For proof they dwell upon what they term its 'feeble trite ideas confined within stiff couplets,' 'the clumsy verse,' the requested 'prayers,' etc.

To all of which it might perhaps be properly urged that this epilogue, like much of the play itself, seems somewhat allegorical; that we must therefore attempt to look beneath the surface; that there are also uncouth verses and harsh-sounding couplets in the play; but if we can find an inner meaning in the epilogue, we may not only pardon the clumsiness, but even say like Milton,

> "Those rugged words to our like mouths grow sleek,
> That would have made Quintilian stare and gasp."

Think of Prospero as Shakespeare himself, bidding farewell, not only to the glorious enchantments of the drama, but to its unspeakable degradations in the hands of other playwrights of that age; a magician who feels that, in spite of himself, his art has not been wholly free from the contamination of those surroundings of which he exclaims, in his one hundred and eleventh sonnet,

> "And almost thence my nature is subdued
> To what it works in, like the dyer's hand!"

He quits his theatre. "Every third thought shall be my grave." His mood is distinctly religious.

Line 3. **most faint**. Has a reaction come? *ennui?* — 6. **dukedom**. What? — 8. **your spell** = imaginary enchantment? fascination of old companionship? — 9. **release ... bands**, etc. Noise broke the spell of

With the help of your good hands. 10
Gentle breath of yours my sails
Must fill, or else my project fails,
Which was to please. Now I want
Spirits to enforce, art to enchant;
And my ending is despair,
Unless I be reliev'd by prayer,
Which pierces so that it assaults
Mercy itself, and frees all faults.
As you from crimes would pardon'd be,
Let your indulgence set me free. 20

---

enchantments. See IV, i, 59. Allegory?— 10. **hands** = hand-clapping? co-operation?—11. **breath,** of applause? of sympathy? of devotion?— 13. **to please.** The mission of the drama to afford amusement, recreation, joy?—15. **despair.** Natural under the circumstances? common to necromancers in their last moments [Warburton]?— Furness's *Var. ed.; As You L. I.,* V, iv, 36, p. 269.— 16. **prayer.** Efficaciously offered for necromancers [Warburton]? prayer for the sovereign offered, according to custom, by players kneeling, at the close of the play [Jephson]? *James,* V, 13, 16.— 17. **assaults.** "The kingdom of Heaven suffereth violence, and the violent take it by force." *Matt.,* xi, 12; *Luke,* xviii, 1-7.— 18. **mercy itself** = divine Mercy? God, the all-merciful?—**frees all faults** = absolves from all sins?— Shakespeare often omits the preposition. Sometimes the construction resembles the Greek accusative, which we translate by supplying in English the words *as to,* or *in regard to. Abbott,* 200.— "Forgiveness and freedom! these are the key-notes of this play."— *Dowden.*

APPENDIX.

HOW TO STUDY ENGLISH LITERATURE.

[*From the Boston Board of School Supervisors*, 1877.]

During the short time given to English Literature in the High Schools, few authors can be studied, and only selections from their works can be critically read. The main purpose, then, of this brief course of study should be to form and cultivate a taste for good literature, to encourage careful and systematic reading, and to illustrate the principles which should guide in selecting authors and works to be read after leaving school. It should be the purpose of the teacher, while keeping the exercises in literature from becoming either mere tasks or pastimes, to make the lessons so interesting that they will be eagerly and vigorously studied, and will inspire a desire for a larger acquaintance with the best authors. This purpose, it is believed, can be accomplished, partly by leading the pupils to perceive the real intent of the author, his thoughts and feelings, the strength of his argument, the beauty and nobleness of his sentiment, and his clear, distinct, forcible, and happy expression; partly by giving a vivid account of his life and times and their influence on each other, and by exciting an interest in the lives of his most eminent literary contemporaries. Thus, by association and comparison, the study of a single author may be an introduction and an incentive to the study of the literature of his period.

. . . .

At the outset, the *whole* of a poem, sketch, essay, or novel should be read by the pupils, either at home or at school. Having formed a general conception of the production, they should study carefully and read intelligently with their teacher those *parts* of it that are most interesting and instructive, and that represent the genius and style of the author.

[*From George H. Martin, Agent of the Mass. Board of Education.*]

What is wanted is a carefully graded course, which, beginning with the poetry of action, should lead the student step by step to the sentimental and the reflective, all in their simplest forms, thence through the more elaborate narrative to the epic and the dramatic. The aim here is not to teach authors or works, but poetry ; and the works are selected for their value as illustrations, without reference to their authors. A parallel course in the study of prose should be pursued with the same end. Then, having learned what poetry is and what prose is, what they contain and how to find their contents, the pupils would be prepared to take up the study of individual authors. Having studied the authors, the final step would be to study the history of the literature, in which the relation of the authors to each other and to their times would appear. This would place the study of literature on a scientific basis, — first elementary ideas, then individual wholes, then relations and classifications.

[*From an address by L. R. Williston, A.M., Supervisor of Public Schools, Boston.*]

How shall the teacher bring his pupils best to see and feel the thoughts of his author as *he* saw and felt them?

First, Read the works carefully with them. Let the teacher read, and question as he reads. Let him often ask for paraphrases, and draw out in every way the thought of his class, making sure that all is clear. Let every *impression* have a corresponding *expression*, which shall re-act, and deepen the impression.

Second, When a part of the work, an act, book, or canto, has been carefully read, assign a theme for a written essay. Let the class tell what the poet has attempted, how he has succeeded, what are the impressions made by the characters, scenes, and descriptions.

Let the teacher himself write upon the themes assigned to his class, and thus give them a model of what he wishes them to do.

Third, When the book or play has been carefully read and studied in this way in all its parts, let it be re-read in a larger and freer way than before. Let the pupils read, and the teacher watch to see if the thought is clearly apprehended by the pupil. Let the fine passages be read again and again by different members of the class, and their rendering be criticised by class and teacher. If the work read be a play, let the parts be taken by different members of the class. Let all the parts of the work now be studied in their relation to each other and to the whole. Essays now should be written upon subjects suggested by this more comprehensive study of the work, — a comparison of characters, noteworthy scenes and their bearing upon the whole, the style of the author, and his skill in description, dramatic presentation, or invention.

Fourth, With the careful reading and study of some book *in school*, I think it important that there should go the reading of some other book *out of* school. Flowers are not all to be picked and analyzed, but are to be enjoyed as they are seen by "him who runs." "Some books are to be tasted, others to be swallowed, some few to be chewed and digested." Let the pupil have his exercise in merely "tasting" books, with enjoyment as the chief end. Let the teacher be his guide, and merely ask him to report what he finds. In other words, let him read, as we all read when we read for pleasure, — with his mind at ease and open to every charm that genius can present. Let the teacher make the book the subject of conversation with his class, and draw their attention by his questions to the chief points which make it noteworthy.

Do not make a disagreeable task of any such exercise. For, that our pupils may receive the highest and best influence from this study of English literature, it is essential that they love it, and retain only pleasant memories of the hours spent at school in the society of its best authors.

[*From J. M. Buchan, Inspector of High Schools, Ontario, Canada: quoted in Blaisdell's "Outline Studies in English Classics."*]

With all classes of pupils alike, the main thing to be aimed at by the teacher is to lead them clearly and fully to understand the meaning of the author they are reading, and to appreciate the beauty, the nobleness, the justness, or the sublimity of his thoughts and language. Parsing, the analysis of sentences, the derivation of words, the explanation of allusions, the scansion of verse, the pointing-out of figures of speech, the hundred and one minor matters on which the teacher may easily dissipate the attention of the pupil, should be strictly subordinated to this great aim. . . . It is essential that the mind of the reader should be put *en rapport* with that of the writer. There is something in the influence of a great soul upon another, which defies analysis. No analysis of a poem, however subtle, can produce the same effect upon the mind and heart as the reading of the poem itself.

[*From F. G. Fleay's "Guide to Chaucer and Spenser."*]

No doubtful critical point should ever be set before the student as ascertained. One great advantage of these studies is the acquirement of a power of forming a judgment in cases of conflicting evidence. Give the student the evidence; state your own opinion, if you like, but let him judge for himself.

No extracts or incomplete works should be used. The capability of appreciating a whole work, as a whole, is one of the principal aims in æsthetic culture.

It is better to read thoroughly one simple play or poem than to know details about all the dramatists and poets. The former trains the brain to judge of other plays or poems: the latter only loads the memory with details that can at any time be found, when required, in books of reference.

For these studies to completely succeed, they must be as thorough as our classical studies used to be. No difficult point in syntax, prosody, accidence, or pronunciation; no variation in manners or customs; no historical or geographical allusion, — must be passed over without explanation. This training in exactness will not interfere with, but aid, the higher aims of literary training.

[*From Blaisdell's "Outlines for the Study of English Classics."*]

The following summary of points to be exacted . . . may prove useful : —

I. — Points relative to substance.
1. A general knowledge of the purport of the passages, and line of argument pursued.
2. An exact paraphrase of parts of the whole, producing exactly and at length the author's meaning.
3. The force and character of epithets.
4. The meaning of similes, and expansions of metaphors.
5. The exact meaning of individual words.

II. — Points with regard to form.
1. General grammar rules; if necessary, peculiarities of English grammar.
2. Derivations: (1) General laws and principles of derivations, including a knowledge of affixes and suffixes. (2) Interesting historical derivation of particular words.

III. — The knowledge of all allusions.

IV. — A knowledge of such parallel passages and illustrations as the teacher has supplied.

From all that has been quoted from the foregoing authorities, it may justly be inferred that somehow or other the pupil must be made to feel an *interest* in the author, to *admire* what is admirable in the composition, and really to ENJOY its study. Secure this, and all else will follow as a matter of course : fail in this, and the time is wasted.

The following suggestions,[1] or some of them, may be helpful in daily class-work : —

1. At the beginning of the exercise, or as often as need be, require a statement of —
   (*a*) The main object of the author in the whole poem, oration, play, or other production of which to-day's lesson is a part.
   (*b*) The object of the author in this particular canto, chapter, act, or other division of the main work.
2. Read or recite from memory (or have the pupils do it) the finest part or parts of the last lesson. The elocutionary talent of the class should be utilized here, so that the author may appear at his best.
3. Require at times (often enough to keep the whole fresh in memory) a *résumé* of the "argument," story, or succession of topics, up to the present lesson.

---

[1] See Suggestions to Teachers, in Sprague's edition of the First Two Books of *Paradise Lost* and *Lycidas;* also in his *Six Selections from Irving.*

APPENDIX.

4. Have the student read aloud the sentence, paragraph, or lines, now (or previously) assigned. The appointed portion should have some unity.
5. Occasionally let the student interpret exactly the meaning by substituting his own words; explain peculiarities. This paraphrase should often be in *writing*.
6. Let him state the immediate object of the author in *these* lines. Is this object relevant? important? appropriate in *this* place?
7. Let him point out the ingredients (particular thoughts) that make up the passage. Are they in good taste? just? natural? well arranged?
8. Let him point out other merits or defects, — anything noteworthy as regards nobleness of principle or sentiment, grace, delicacy, beauty, rhythm, sublimity, wit, wisdom, humor, *naiveté*, kindliness, pathos, energy, concentrated truth, logical force, originality; give allusions, kindred passages, principles illustrated, etc.

The choicest passages may be made the basis of language study, in accordance with the foregoing suggestions, somewhat as follows (Act IV, sc. i, 148-159): —

1. *Repeat from memory, with proper expression*, this passage, —

> Our revels now are ended. These our actors,
> As I foretold you, were all spirits, and
> Are melted into air, into thin air:
> And, like the baseless fabric of this vision,
> The cloud-capp'd towers, the gorgeous palaces,
> The solemn temples, the great globe itself,
> Yea, all which it inherit, shall dissolve,
> And, like this insubstantial pageant faded,
> Leave not a rack behind. We are such stuff
> As dreams are made on; and our little life
> Is rounded with a sleep.

2. *Comment* on particular words and sentences.

In this passage 'revels' may be from Lat. *rebellare*, to rebel, influenced in meaning perhaps by Fr. *réveiller*, to awake, fr. Lat. *re*, again, *ex*, out, *vigilare*, to wake.

'Foretold' is *told before* (in line 120). 'Spirits,' as the etymology of the word suggests, from *spirare*, to breathe, are of the *air* and return to *air*. The word well illustrates the physical basis or analogy which commonly underlies all our vocabulary of the supernatural. 'Into thin air,' is an evident recollection of Virgil's *in tenuem auram*, *Æneid*, iv, 278. 'Palaces' are so called originally from the splendid residences erected by the Cæsars and others upon the Palatine Mount at Rome. 'Solemn,'. Old Lat. *solus* (for *totus*, entire) and *annus*, a year, originally meant happening but once in a whole year, anniversary, and therefore important, momentous. 'Globe' may mean the universe, the celestial, as well as the terrestrial sphere; but is generally supposed to mean here our earth. Gr. γλόβος, Lat. *globus*.

'Inherit' is used, as elsewhere in Shakespeare, for *possess*. 'Pageant' is from Lat. *compaginata*, framed together, *pangere*, base *pag*, to fasten, put together, to frame, to construct. A pageant in Shakespeare's time signified a magnificent spectacle exhibited upon a great framework. See *Mer. of Ven.*, I, i, 11.

'Rack' is etymologically the same with *wrack* (*wreck*), something *drifted* ashore, or *drifting;* from Icel. *rek*, drift. In Shakespeare it is perhaps a fragmentary cloud, precursor or relic of a storm. Moore's verses in *The Fire-Worshippers* (in *Lalla Rookh*) well illustrate the sense: —

> The day is lowering; stilly black
> Sleeps the grim wave, while heaven's *rack*,
> Dispersed and wild, twixt earth and sky,
> Hangs like a shattered canopy.
> There's not a cloud in that blue plain
> But tells of storm to come or past,
> Here flying loosely as the mane
> Of a young war-horse in the blast,
> There rolled in masses dark and swelling,
> As proud to be the thunder's dwelling,
> While some, already burst and riven,
> Seem melting down the verge of heaven.

'Stuff,' for material, seems used with slight disparagement, due, perhaps, in part, to the expulsive sound with which it must be enunciated.

'Rounded with a sleep.' This is variously interpreted. The circle of life begins and ends with sleep. Says Darmesteter (*Introduction*, p. xxxii), "*Nos petites vies sont les isles du sommeil.*" 'Rounded' is 'finished off as with a crown,' says Wright. Meiklejohn quotes

> Our life is a watch and a vision
> Between a sleep and a sleep.

See in Carlyle's *Sartor Resartus* the paragraph beginning, "We sit as in a boundless phantasmagoria or dream grotto"; and in *Julius Cæsar*, V, iii, 23–25, —

> This day I breathed first; time is come round,
> And where I did begin, there shall I end.
> My life is run his compass.

Douglas Campbell (*Puritans in England, Holland, and America*) and some others hastily infer from this passage that Shakespeare was an atheist, or infidel, or at least a disbeliever in the immortality of the soul. But the language of Prospero in Act I, Sc. ii, 159, of Ariel, Act III, Sc. iii, 70–82, the Prayer referred to in the Epilogue, and the explicit declaration in Shakespeare's Will, strongly tend to a different conclusion.

3. *Translate* into different English words.

Our fantastic sports at length are finished. All these play-performers of ours, as I previously declared to you, were beings incorporeal, and are dissolved into mere atmosphere, attenuated atmosphere. Similarly to this spectacle's foundationless structure, too, the turrets whose heads are crowned with sky-mist, the rich and splendid houses of the great, the awe-inspiring edifices of the gods, the vast round world itself — yes, everything which possesses it — shall melt away, and, like dissolving views of this magnificent show without substance, vanish, with not a film of cloud in the welkin to tell that they have ever been. We are such matter as constitutes the imaginings of one in sleep, and our petty existence is encircled with slumber.

We have Shakespeare's maturest thoughts. He seems to think, with Professor Langley, so universes *come and go.*

Criticism from the class should be called for, corrections should be made by the instructor, and parallel passages should be quoted.

Such treatment of choice passages, often thoroughly memorized and recited with proper *elocutionary expression*, should sometimes be mainly in writing. However imperfect, it gives in large measure that kind of drill which the best training in Latin and Greek imparts. Its importance as a mental discipline, an enlargement of the student's vocabulary, a cultivation of the taste, an acquisition of rich and fruitful treasures of thought, and a means of securing both facility and felicity of expression, can hardly be overestimated.

SPECIMEN OF EXAMINATION PAPERS.

Taken in part from the Papers of the English Civil Service Commission. Perhaps too much attention is paid in them to *phraseology*.

A (First Act chiefly)

1. Give the substance of the story told by Prospero to Miranda.
2. State the parts played by Ariel and Caliban; the history of each.
3. State by whom, to whom, and on what occasions the following lines were uttered: —

   (a) We are *merely* cheated of our lives by drunkards
   (b) In the dark *backward* and *abysm* of time.
   (c) From the *still-vex'd Bermoothēs*, there she's hid.
   (d) To do *me business* in the veins o' the earth.
   (e) He's *gentle* and not *fearful.*
   (f) A *single* thing, as I am now, that wonders.
   (g) What *cares* these roarers for the name of king?

4. Explain the words in Italics in the above.
5. Explain Shakespeare's use of the following words and phrases: (a) *Play the man;* (b) *incharitable;* (c) *god of power;* (d) *the very virtue;* (e) *holp;* (f) *from such a deed;* (g) *closeness;* (h) *a hint that wrings mine eyes;* (i) *grand hests;* (j) *capable of.*
5. Give some instances of Shakespeare's peculiar grammar in the use of double comparatives and such phrases as *I were best.*

B (Second Act).

1. Give a brief account of the action in the Second Act.
2. State the substance of the passage quoted by Gonzalo from Montaigne; its bearing on the date of composition.
3. State by whom, to whom, and on what occasions the following lines were uttered: —

   (a) I saw him beat the *surges* under him.
   (b) *Bourn,* bound of land, *tilth,* vineyard, none.

(c) To the perpetual *wink* for aye might put.
(d) They will not give a *doit* to relieve a lame beggar.
(e) Misery acquaints a man with strange bedfellows.

4. Explain the words in Italics in the above.
5. Annotate and explain the peculiarities in the following words and phrases: (a) *A paragon to their queen;* (b) *the dear'st of the loss;* (c) *minister occasion;* (d) *ebbing men;* (e) *candied;* (f) *sudden;* (g) *inchmeal;* (h) *after the wisest;* (i) *overblown;* (j) *an eye of green.*
6. Give some instances of Shakespeare's compounds with *un.*

C (Third Act).

1. Give a short account of the conversation in Scene i.
2. Contrast the two conspiracies formed by the courtiers and by some of the sailors respectively.
3. By whom, and on what occasions, were the following lines uttered: —

(a) Most busy, *least,* when I do it.
(b) Thou shalt be my lieutenant or my *standard.*
(c) Here's a maze trod, indeed,
Through *forthrights* and *meanders.*
(d) Each *putter-out of five for one* will bring us.
(e) With *good life*
And *observation strange,* my meaner ministers
Their several kinds have done.

4. Explain the words in Italics.
5. Explain fully Shakespeare's use of the following words and phrases: (a) *Sore;* (b) *the top of admiration;* (c) *plain;* (d) *brained like us;* (e) *to paunch;* (f) *brave;* (g) *gentle-kind;* (h) *ecstasy;* (i) *burn but his books.*
6. Annotate any irregularities in Shakespeare's grammar you may have noticed in the Third Act.

D (Fourth Act).

1. Quote the speech beginning, 'Our revels now are ended.' Point out its merits.
2. State by whom, and on what occasions, the following lines were uttered:—

(a) Do not smile at me that *I boast her off.*
(b) You nymphs called *Naiads* of the wandering brooks.
(c) 'Steal by line and level,' is an excellent *pass of pate.*
(d) Being *lass-lorn;* thy *pole-clipt vineyard.*

3. Explain and annotate the words in Italics.
4. Explain fully Shakespeare's use of the following words and phrases: (a) *Fairly;* (b) *freely;* (c) *wonder'd;* (d) *distempered;* (e) *meet with;* (f) *hoodwink this mischance;* (g) *aged cramps;* (h) *villanous low;* (i) *rounded with a sleep.*
5. Quote a few instances of Shakespeare's use of the word *rack.*
6. Give some instances of the irregularities of Shakespeare's verse in *The Tempest.*

E (Fifth Act chiefly).

1. What event reconciles the opposing parties and differing circumstances? And how?
2. Quote Gonzalo's summing up of the play.

APPENDIX. 141

3. State by whom, and on what occasions, the following lines were uttered: —
   (a) In the lime-grove which *weather-fends* your cell.
   (b) Destiny that hath *to instrument* this lower world.
   (c) Bravely, *my diligence*. Thou shalt be free.
   (d) And deal in her command *without* her power.
   (e) Mine would, sir, were I human.
4. Explain fully the words in Italics.
5. Annotate and explain Shakespeare's use of the following words and phrases: (a) *His carriage;* (b) *high wrongs;* (c) *fancy;* (d) *sir;* (e) *remorse and nature;* (f) *taste;* (g) *do offices of truth;* (h) *resolve you.*
6. Give some instances of Shakespeare's use of the abstract for the concrete, and of the concrete for the abstract.
7. State what you know of the sources of *The Tempest.*

SOME TOPICS FOR ESSAYS.

Most poor matters point to rich ends, III, i, 3, 4.
Most busy least, III, i, 15.
Shakespeare's knowledge of navigation.
Caliban 'the missing link.'
Magic, necromancy, hypnotism.
Prospero's life in Milan.
Prospero's life on the island.
The Bermudas.
Shakespeare's geography.
Difficulties in creating Ariel's personality.
Difficulties in creating Miranda's personality.
Same in the case of Caliban.
Story of the the first scene.
Story of Act III, sc. iii.
Story of the conspiracy, II, i.
Story of the conspiracy, III, ii; IV, i.
Probable origin of the play.
Use of prose and blank verse in the play.
'End-stopt' and 'run-on' lines.
Every man shift for all the rest, etc., V, i, 256, 257 (altruism?).
What does Prospero typify?
Forgiveness in Act V.
Observance of the 'unities.'
Didactic purpose in the play?
Trinculo.
Court jesters.
Ariel and electricity.
Stephano and drunkenness.
Is Prospero Shakespeare?
St. Elmo's fire.
Prospero as teacher, I, ii, 172.
Miranda as teacher, I, ii, 352.
Importance attached to books, I, ii, 109, 166–168; III, i, 94; III, ii, 85, 88, 91; V, i, 57.
'Destiny that hath to instrument this lower world,' III, iii, 53, 54.
Allegory in the play. See *Dowden*, pp. 377–380.
Deities as elementary powers.
'The Powers delaying not forgetting,' III, iii, 73.
Wendell's suggestion of Shakespeare's 'decadence.'
Classical learning in the play.
Ferdinand and Miranda in III, i.
Gonzalo.
Sycorax and Setebos.
Browning's '*Caliban on Setebos.*'
Evanescence, IV, ii, 154–157.
Astrology, I, ii, 180–184.
Contrasts in the play.
'Nothing of him that doth fade But doth suffer a sea change,' etc., I, ii, 398–400.
Function of each act in the drama. (See Freytag's *Technique of the Drama.*)

INDEX.

A

abbreviations, 22
abstemious, 103
abuse, 120
abysm, 83
ache, 92
aches (or *aitches?*), 52
admire, 122
advantage, 27
adventure . . . weakly, 66
afore, 76, 100
after (= afterwards?), 73
again, 53
aged cramps, 118
a-hold, 23
Alexandrine line, 37
allegory, 130, 131
alliteration, 53
amain, 104
Amphion, 62
an (= if?), 66
and if, 120
Appendix, 132–141
are (in 'coral are'), 53
Argier, 46
Ariel, 13, 42, 43, etc.
arise, 41
arts, liberal, 35
aspersion, 101
assist the storm, 26
attach'd (= attacked?), 93
attend, 56
avoid, 108
awak'd, 87
aye, for, 71
azur'd vault, 117

B

backward, 33
badges, 127
barnacles, 113
bass my trespass, 98
bate, 45, 62
bat-fowling, 66
Baynes, 104
be (plural?), 70, 81
bear up, 86
beating, 41, 126
Beaumont & Fletcher, 29
become, 90
Bermoothes, 44
Bermudas, 10, 44
berries, water with (coffee?), 50
besides, 84
best, thou 'rt, 51
bestow, 129
betid, 88
bigger light, 50
blow, 84
blue-ey'd, 47
board 'em, 86
boatswain, 25
boded, 85
boiled, 117
bombard, 74
book, 86, 90, 117
bootless, 83
bosky, 105
boson, 26
bourn, 65
brained, 87, 90
brave, 81, 55, 90
braver, more, 55
bravely, 97
breath, 131
bring her to try, 28
broom groves, 104
brown (or 'broom'), 30
Browning, Robert, 20
budge, 115
burthen, 52
but, 54
but doubt discovery, 69
butt, 39, 77
by and by, 92

C

Caliban, 12, 13, 16, etc.
Campbell, 14.
can, 101
candied, 70
canker, 54
cares (for 'care'?), 27
carriage, 115
case, 87
cast, 69
cat o' mountain, 113
catch, 91
certes, 94
chalk'd forth, 124
chaps, 76
cheek, welkin's, 31
cheer, 25
cheerly, 26
cherubin, 40
chess, 122
chirurgeonly, 64
chough, 70
cockerel, 60
coffee, 50
coil, 43
Coleridge, 13, 80, 86, 95
come by, 71
composite masterpiece, 84
condition, 38
conduct, 126
confederates, 38
confines, 107
consent, 67
constant, 43
content, 70
contrary, 37
control, 55
cooling . . . with sighs, 44
coragio, 127
coral made, 53
corollary, 108
correspondent, 48
courses, 28
Cowden-Clarke, 46
crabs, 79
cram, 63
creature (collective?), 31
crisp, 107
critical comments, 11
curfew, 117
curtsied (or 'courtesied'), 52

D

-*d*, or -*ed* (omitted suffix), 36, 40
Dagon, 49
dalliance, 103
date of composition of play, 9
dead Indian, 74
dear, 121
dearest, 64
debosh'd, 87
decadence (of Shakespeare's powers?), 21
deck'd the sea, 40
deliver'd, 60, 129
demi-puppets, 116
demoniacal possession (sign of?), 76
devour, 122

144   INDEX.

devouring, 97
dew-lapp'd, 95
Dido, 62
Die Schöne Sidea, 11
diligent ear, 83
Dis, 105
disease, 118
discharges, electric, 43
discovers, 122
distinctly (= separately ?), 43
doit, 74
dollar ... dolor, 60
doth, 27
double comparative, 55, 101
dove-drawn, 105
Dowden, 103, 115
dowle, 96
down, unshrubb'd, 105
drawn, 72, 78
drink the air, 119
drollery, 93
drowning mark, 27
Dryden, 11

E

ecstasy, 99
edge, 102
electric lights, 43
Elmo's fire, St., 43
elves, 116
enchanted trifle, 120
end o' th' beam, 63
engine, 65
Eng. Literature (study of), 132–141
envy, 46
Epilogue, 130
ere, or, 82
essays, topics for, 141
estate, 105
event, 88, 85
ever, or, 41
execution of pirates, 29
eye of green, 61

F

face, 37
fall it, 71
fathom, 53
fear me, 128
fearful, 57
feater, 70
featly, 52
fellow, 85
fellowly, 118
fends, 115
Ferdinand, 19, 43, 108, etc.
few, in (Lat. idiom ?), 39
fire (dissyl. ?), 31
five for one, 95
flat-long, 66
Florio's Montaigne, 64
flote, 44
foil, 83
foison, 65, 106

fool to weep, 85
footing, 108
for (= in respect to ?), 28
forego, 93
foreheads, 113
foretold, 108
forgiveness and freedom, 131
forth-rights, 92
founder'd, 102
Franz Horn, 45
fraughting, 32
frees (= frees from ?), 131
freshes, the quick, 89
fringed curtains, 54
frippery, 112
from (peculiar sense of), 34
frustrate, 93
full poor, 32
Furness, 20, *et passim*
Furnivall, 17
furze, 80, 110

G

gaberdine, 75, 77
gait, Juno's, 106
gallant, 54
gallows, perfect, 27
garments, sustaining, 44
Garnett, 19, 31
gave out, 125
genius, worser, 101
gentle, 57
gently, 48
gilded, 128
glasses, 45, 125
glut, 29
go (= walk ?), 87
go to, 113
golden age, 65
Golding's Ovid, 116
Gonzalo, good, 27, *et passim*
good (how used ?), 25, 27, 111
good life, 97
goodly, 123
goose, 78
gorse, 110
green sour ringlets, 116
grind their joints, 118
grudge, 45

H

hair, 112
Hakluyt's Voyages, 43
hand, 27
hand, by this, 88, 112
hap, 27
harpy, 95, 96, 97
Hazlitt, 12
he (in 'of he or Adrian,'), 60
hearkens (transitive ?), 88
hearts, 26
heath, 80

heavy (proleptic ?), 66
Heine, 14
Heraud, 48
hests, 47
high-day (or hey-day ?), 80
hint, 39, 59
hollowly, 85
holp, 34
Holt, John, 11
home (= completely ?), 113
honeycomb, 50
hoodwink, 111
Hudson, Rev. H., 13
Hugo, 15
Hymen, 101, 105

I

I (omitted), 52
ignorant (= of ignorance ?), 113
impertinent, 39
incharitable, 28
inch-meal, 78
infest, 126
in few (Lat. *paucis* ?), 39
influence, 42
inherit, 79, 108
inquisition, bootless, 33
instrument, to, 96
into (for ' in ' ?), 47, 51
into truth, 37
Irving Shakespeare, 19, 31
is (for ' are ' ?), 57, 125
it (for ' its ' ?), 65
it's (peculiar form), 37, 53
ivy (parasitic ?), 36

J

Jack, played the, 111
Jameson, Mrs., 13
jerkin, 112
Johnson, Samuel, 12
Jove's stout oak, 117
justify (prove or convict ?), 120

K

keep (= stay, live ?), 70
Kemble, Mrs., 13, 97
key, 36
keynotes of the play, 131
kibe, 70
-kin (in ' lakin '), 92
kinds, 98
knock a nail, 89
knot, 44

L

lakin, 92
lass-lorn, 104
Latin idiom, 39
learning (transitive ?), 51
lie there, my art, 32
lieu o' the premises, 38

life, with good, 97
like (= alike ?), 96
like of, 84
line, 110, 112
line and level, 112
line-grove, 115
ling (or 'long' ?), 80
list, 87, 91
liver, 103
Lloyd, 14
long (or 'ling' ?), 80
lord, good my, 111
lorded, 87
Lowell, J. R., 16
lush, 61
lust, 101
Lusty, 61

M

mad, of the, 43
made on, 109
maid, 55
maid (servant ?), 85
main-course, 28
make a man, 74
malignant spirits, 46
manacle, 56
manage, 35
man in the moon, 69, 78
man's life, 69
mantle, 118
mantled, 110
marmoset, 79
marr'd, 107
marry, 83
Martin, Lady, 20
masque in Act IV., 11, 114
massy, 83
master of vessel, 25
masterpiece, composite, 84
masters, weak, 117
Max Müller, 113
meanders, 92
meaner, 98
meddle with, 32
merely, 29
messenger of Juno, 104
mettle, 66
might (= could ?), 38
minion, 105
ministers, 89
Miranda, 13, 16, 17, etc.
miss (peculiar sense ?), 48
missing link, 114, 127
moe, 64
mole, blind, 111
momentary, 43
Montégut, 15
moon-calf, 77
mop and mow, 102
moping, 126
more braver, 55
most busy, least, 61
most poor, 61
mount, 78
mouths, cold, 29

mow, 73
mows, 97
Mulgrave, Lord, 28, 30
mum, 88
murkiest, 101
murrain, 89
muse, 94
my lord, good, 111

N

Naiads, 107
nail, knock a, 89
Naples, I am, 55
natural, 87
Nausicaa, 17
neat's leather, 76
negative (double), 54
Neptune, 43, 116
nerves, 58
nimble lungs, 65
ninny, 89
Nobody, picture of, 91
nonpareil, 90
nor no, 54
noise (breaks spells ?), 130
not bites, 117
not doubt, 63
not know, 120
note (= information or letter ?), 69
nuptial, 129

O

oar'd, 63
observation strange, 98
occasion, 67
odd, 127
odd angle, 44
o'erpriz'd 36
off and on, 87
of power (= powerful ?), 32
of whence, 82
office (= official voice ?), 28
of (= about, in 'study of' ?), 62
of (= in, in 'dead of sleep' ?), 126
of (= redundant, in 'cooling of' ?), 44
old (= huge, old-fashioned ?), 51
omit, 42, 66
on (for 'of' ?), 109
on't, 36, 51, 56, 63
ooze, 45
opportune (accent ?), 101
or ere (= before ever ?), 82, 116
out (= past ?), 33
Ovid, 116
owed, 88
owes, 54
owest, 56
owl and bat, 119

P

pageant, 109
painful (sports), 81
pains, 45
Paphos, 105
paragon, 61
pard, 113
pass of pate, 112
passion, 63, 116
patch, 89
pate, 112
paunch, 90
peacocks (Juno's), 104
perpetual, 71
pertly, 103
Phillpotts, 17, 80
Phœbus, 102
phœnix, 94
picture of Nobody, 91
piece of virtue, 84
pied, 89
pig-nuts, 79
pioned, 103
plague, the red, 51
plantation, 64
play the men, 26
pluck, 120
point (= have a view, tend, aim at ?), 81
point, to, 42
pole-clipt, 104
poor-john, 74
positions of the ship, 30
post, 69
power, god of, 32
praise in departing, 95
prayer (efficacy of ?), 131
premises (law term ?), 88
prerogative, 37
present, peace of the, 27
presented (= acted ?), 109
presently, 38, 119
princess (plural ?), 41
printless foot, 116
probable, 126
proper, 75
prose, and blank verse, 30, 72
Prospero, 14, 16, 19, *et passim*
Prospero (= Shakespeare ?), 115
Providence divine, 40
provision (or 'prevision' ?), 83
puppy-headed monster, 78
putter-out of five for one, 95

Q

quaint, 49
quality, 42
quick freshes, 89
quit, 39, 40

R

rack, 109
Raleigh, Walter, 28
rankest, 121
rapt, 35
rate, 36, 63
reasonable (= of reason ?), 118
red plague rid you, 51
reeling ripe, 128
rein (to give the rein), 103
relish, 116
remember (= remind of ?), 53
remorse (= tender feeling, pity ?), 118
requit, 97
resolve, 126
retire me, 129
revenue, 37
rid (= thrust away, destroy ?), 51
right out, 106
ringlets, 117
roarers, 27
rounded, 109
Russel, 17

S

sack (sherry ?), 77, 89
safe, 82
safely (for 'safe' ?), 125
saffron, 105
Saint Elmo's fire, 43
sanctimonious, 101
sans, 37
scamels, 79
scaped, 75
Schlegel, 12, 49
schoolmaster, 41
score (= stake ? twenty ?), 128
scurvy, 75
sea-marge, 104
sedg'd, 107
sensible, 65
servant-monster, 86
set (= fixed ?), 87
Setebos, 127
sets off, 81
several, 83, 126
shak'd, 72
Shakespeare's technical knowledge of seamanship, 30, 45, 125
she (for 'her' ?), 90
should (peculiar use ?), 53, 67, 71
shouldst, 67
shroud (= take shelter ?), 75
signiories, 35
single, 55, 126
skilless, 84
skottowe, 13

Smith, Capt. John, 25, 28
so (ellipsis of ?), 36, 52, 92
sociable to the show, 118
soft (= stop, go slowly ?), 56
solemnized, 129
Somers, Sir George, 10
something (adverb ?), 54, 84
sometime, 118
sore, 128
sort, 62, 108
sot, 90
source of the plot, 10
southwest (wind ?), 49
speak, 25
sphere, 66
spongy, 104
sprites, 77
spriting, 48
St. Elmo's fire, 43
stained, 61
stale, 110
standard, 87
staring (in 'upstaring'), 43
state, 35
steaded, 41
still (= always ?), 124, 133
still-closing, 96
stock-fish, 89
stomach, an undergoing, 40, 63
stover, 108
Strachey, Sir E., 54
Study of Eng. Lit., 132–141
subtleties, 120
suffered (= suffered death?), 74
suggestion, 71
sun sucks up, 73
supportable (accent ?), 121
swabber, 75
Sycorax, 46, 90

T

tabor, 91
tang, 75
tawny, 61
teen, 34
tell (= count ?), 59, 71
temperance (= temperature ?), 60
Tempest (last written play ?), 14, 15, 16
temple, 56
tended, 88
tender, 70
text of the play, 9
th (sense of suffix), 64
that (= provided that ?), 122
that (= so that ?), 36, 52, 92
that (omitted after 'but' ?), 54
that's verily, 72
the man in the moon, 69, 78
thee (and 'thou'. Difference ?), 118
thick, 50

thin air (= *tenuem auram*?), 108
third (or 'thrid' or 'thread' ?), 100
thought, with a, 109
throes, 68
throughly, 93
tilth, 65
to (= 'as' or 'for' ?), 61, 96
to (= as to ?), 65
to point, 42
tooth'd, 110
topics for essays, 141
topmast, down with the, 28
top of admiration, 88
topsail, 26
tortoise, 49
trash, 35, 36, 112
trebles thee, 67
trembling (sign of demoniacal possession ?), 76
trenchering, 80
tricksy, 126
trident, 43
troll, 91
trumpery, 110
try with the main-course, 28
Tunis, 62
twangling instruments, 92
twelve year since, 84
twilled brims, 103
twink, 102

U

unback'd, 110
undergoing stomach, 40
unities (in the drama), 9
urchins, 50, 78
utensils (accent ?), 90

V

vanity, 102
vast of night, 50
verily, that's, 72
verse tests, 9, 10
vetches, 108
villanous, 113
vineyard (syllabication ?), 104
virgin-knot, 101
virtue (peculiar sense ?), 32
visitor, 59
vouchsafe, 55

W

waist (of ship ?), 43
wallets, 95
ward, 57
wardrobe, 112
washing of ten tides, 29
wearily (for 'weary' ?), 82
weasand, 90

weather (= storm ?), 28
weather-fends, 115
weigh'd, 63
welkin, 31
wench, 39
Wendell, B., 20, 129, 130
which end o' th' beam, 63
which (for 'who'?), 81
while-ere, 91
whist, 52
whistle, master's, 26
White, R. G., 19
who (inflection neglected?), 35
who (= which ?), 31
who (*nominativus pendens?*), 94
whom . . . is, 98

whoreson, 28
wicked dew, 49
wide-chapped, 29
will (expressing repetition in 'will hum'?), 92
Wilson, D., 114
winding, 107
winkst, 67
without (= beyond ?), 127
woe, 121
woe the day, 32
worser genius, 101
would (expressing repetition in 'I'd divide'), 43
wound, 73
wrack, 82
wrangle, 123
wraths, 97

wrongs (= sins, offences ?), 120

Y

yare, 26, 125
yarely, 25
ye, content, 122
year (for 'years'?), 34
yond, 54
you (and 'thou'. Difference.), 34
Young's *Night Thoughts*, 66

Z

zenith, 42

www.ingramcontent.com/pod-product-compliance
Lightning Source LLC
Chambersburg PA
CBHW030355170426
43202CB00010B/1381